CONTENTS

OPENING STATEMENTS

PRESS RELEASE

PUBLIC WITNESSES

ALPHABETICAL LISTING AND APPENDIX MATERIAL SUBMITTED

S. HRG. 103–1027

SPECIAL 301 TRADE REMEDY

HEARING

BEFORE THE

SUBCOMMITTEE ON INTERNATIONAL TRADE

OF THE

COMMITTEE ON FINANCE
UNITED STATES SENATE

ONE HUNDRED THIRD CONGRESS

SECOND SESSION

JUNE 24, 1994

Printed for the use of the Committee on Finance

U.S. GOVERNMENT PRINTING OFFICE

88–739—CC WASHINGTON : 1994

For sale by the U.S. Government Printing Office
Superintendent of Documents, Congressional Sales Office, Washington, DC 20402
ISBN 0-16-047078-1

COMMITTEE ON FINANCE

DANIEL PATRICK MOYNIHAN, New York, *Chairman*

MAX BAUCUS, Montana
DAVID L. BOREN, Oklahoma
BILL BRADLEY, New Jersey
GEORGE J. MITCHELL, Maine
DAVID PRYOR, Arkansas
DONALD W. RIEGLE, Jr., Michigan
JOHN D. ROCKEFELLER IV, West Virginia
TOM DASCHLE, South Dakota
JOHN B. BREAUX, Louisiana
KENT CONRAD, North Dakota

BOB PACKWOOD, Oregon
BOB DOLE, Kansas
WILLIAM V. ROTH, Jr., Delaware
JOHN C. DANFORTH, Missouri
JOHN H. CHAFEE, Rhode Island
DAVE DURENBERGER, Minnesota
CHARLES E. GRASSLEY, Iowa
ORRIN G. HATCH, Utah
MALCOLM WALLOP, Wyoming

Lawrence O'Donnell, Jr., *Staff Director*
Lindy L. Paull, *Minority Staff Director and Chief Counsel*

Subcommittee on International Trade

MAX BAUCUS, Montana, *Chairman*

DANIEL PATRICK MOYNIHAN, New York
DAVID L. BOREN, Oklahoma
BILL BRADLEY, New Jersey
GEORGE J. MITCHELL, Maine
DONALD W. RIEGLE, Jr., Michigan
JOHN D. ROCKEFELLER IV, West Virginia
TOM DASCHLE, South Dakota
JOHN B. BREAUX, Louisiana
KENT CONRAD, North Dakota

JOHN C. DANFORTH, Missouri
BOB PACKWOOD, Oregon
WILLIAM V. ROTH, Jr., Delaware
JOHN H. CHAFEE, Rhode Island
CHARLES E. GRASSLEY, Iowa
ORRIN G. HATCH, Utah
MALCOLM WALLOP, Wyoming

SPECIAL 301 TRADE REMEDY

FRIDAY, JUNE 24, 1994

U.S. SENATE,
COMMITTEE ON FINANCE,
SUBCOMMITTEE ON INTERNATIONAL TRADE,
Washington, DC.

The hearing was convened, pursuant to notice, at 2:05 p.m., in room SD–215, Dirksen Senate Office Building, Hon. Max Baucus, Chairman of the Subcommittee, presiding.

Also present: Senator Roth.

[The press release announcing the hearing follows:]

[Press Release No. H–41, June 21, 1994]

INTERNATIONAL TRADE SUBCOMMITTEE SCHEDULES HEARING ON SPECIAL 301 TRADE REMEDY

WASHINGTON, DC—Senator Max Baucus (D–MT), Chairman of the Senate Finance Committee's Subcommittee on International Trade, announced today that the Subcommittee will hold a hearing in advance of the Administration's decision on the designation of "priority foreign countries" under the "Special 301" trade remedy law.

The hearing is scheduled for *Friday, June 24, 1994, at 10:00 a.m.* in room SD–215 of the Dirksen Senate Office Building.

Senator Baucus said, "Special 301 is a critical law that ensures respect for the works of American artists, authors, software engineers and inventors worldwide. This hearing will examine the Clinton Administration's implementation of the law, and answer questions about the prospects for the law after the creation of the World Trade Organization."

Under Special 301 (section 182 of the Trade Act of 1974, which was added to the law by the Omnibus Trade and Competitiveness Act of 1988), the U.S. Trade Representative (USTR) is required to identify by the end of April every year those countries that deny adequate and effective protection of intellectual property rights. USTR must also identify which of the cited countries are "priority" countries. Special 301 requires USTR to initiate section 301 investigations, on an accelerated basis, on the practices of the "priority" countries.

On April 30, 1994, United States Trade Representative Mickey Kantor identified 36 countries under the Special 301 provision. USTR Kantor stated that there is consensus that three of the identified countries—Argentina, China, and India—pose the most significant problems. Kantor announced that if a solution to U.S. concerns with these countries is not reached by June 30, 1994, they will be named "priority foreign countries" and investigations of their practices will be initiated.

OPENING STATEMENT OF HON. MAX BAUCUS, A U.S. SENATOR FROM MONTANA, CHAIRMAN OF THE SUBCOMMITTEE

Senator BAUCUS. Good afternoon. The hearing will come to order. We are here this afternoon to discuss the implementation of Special 301 and its implementation over the last year as well as the implications of the new GATT Agreement for Special 301.

Intellectual property industries are among the most successful sectors of our economy. American music, movies, computer software, new machines in medicine contribute widely to our economic growth and balance of trade. They also show our country at its creative and inventive best.

Our health harbor depends on vigilant government action to ensure respect for copyrights, patents and trademarks. For the past 6 years we have used Special 301 as our weapon of last resort in this battle. The law has brought us notable successes all around the world—in China, in Thailand, Brazil, Paraguay and many other countries. It has worked very well over the years.

But this year two serious questions about it have emerged. The first arises in respect to implementation of the basic statute. Special 301 requires the United States to name the worst violators of intellectual property rights on April 30 of each year.

We set a deadline because in any relationship with a foreign country we have many issues on the table—security ties, narcotics, human rights, diplomatic crisis and so on. They are all very important. And as we pursue our goals in these areas, we are always tempted to put off our trade disputes until later.

By requiring a mandatory annual listing, we hope to solve this chronic problem and separate intellectual property protection from foreign policy. Every year we would choose our intellectual property priorities by finding out which countries were doing the least to stop piracy and erecting the most egregious barriers to trade. Nothing more.

This year the People's Republic of China presented us with our most serious problem. An earlier listing of China under Special 301 forced China to adopt modern copyright, patent and trademark laws. But in the copyright area in particular China had done virtually nothing to enforce the law.

As a consequence copyright piracy in China is worsening by the day. China now hosts at least 26 pirate plants which can put out 50 million CDs a year. Software pirates are springing up like little poisonous mushrooms. Videos, books and other products are all in danger.

The International Intellectual Property Association estimates that Chinese piracy costs us $827 million last year, nearly doubling the $415 million figure for 1992. But even worse, the pirates are beginning to compete with our legitimate industries in other Asian markets, in Latin American and even here in the United States.

The fever extends from internationally famous giants like MicroSoft to companies as small as Big Sky Carvers near Bozeman, Montana. This is a brilliant little company. This year, in fact, it won an award as Montana's top small business. It makes ornamental wooden sculptures and hunting decoys and employs about 50 people.

Last fall it found a Chinese company stealing their designs and advertising the pirate product in Louisiana Sportsmen Magazine.

China clearly earned a listing. But when April 30 arrived, we got a rather surprising decision. Rather than list China as a priority foreign country, the administration chose to given them a warning and a 2-month extension until June 30. They did the same favor with Argentina and India, with whom we have very long-standing disputes over patent law.

In the case of China, the reprieve was evidently due to the fear that a priority foreign country listing might upset the Chinese Government. Some may have worried that a listing might make China less willing to give concessions on human rights as the decision on MFN status approached.

That fear seems to have been misplaced, since the delay got us no human rights concessions. And I am not aware of any reason for the delay in listing India and Argentina.

In and of itself the 2-month extension does us no critical damage, but it sets a very disturbing precedent. In my view, it throws the annual deadline into Special 301 into question. We are now left to wonder whether the deadlines will be met and the law enforced in the future or whether foreign policy considerations have crept back into the process and will once again take precedence over clear and compelling cases of abusive trade practices in foreign countries.

I had hoped to put these questions to rest in this hearing. But to my regret the administration has chosen not to provide us with a witness today. My staff was told that, since delicate negotiations are underway, this is not a good time for a hearing.

The first assertion is true. During my 20 years in Congress we have always had some sort of delicate negotiations underway, but that has not generally prevented hearings. So I am a bit puzzled and disappointed that the administration will not participate today.

The second issue, of course, is the implication of the new World Trade Organization for Special 301. The WTO for the first time sets international rules for protecting intellectual property. It also gives countries with weaker standards some time to phase in new laws and complicates trade retaliation by binding tariffs on a larger number of products.

In my view these problems can be solved in implementing legislation. We must make sure Special 301 can be used to seek full enforcement of GATT commitments and speed up the phase-in of new and stronger laws. It must also require careful monitoring of country's adherence to WTO standards and mandate U.S. action if they are not met.

We should consider all the tools we have, such as withdrawing or suspending GSP and foreign aid to countries which allow piracy of American works. Today we will get the views of three critical industries—music, pharmaceuticals and software—on all these issues. And we are very privileged to have three very knowledgeable witnesses who can help us begin to resolve these issues.

I would like to turn to Senator Roth, from Delaware, for any statement he may wish to have.

OPENING STATEMENT OF HON. WILLIAM V. ROTH, JR., A U.S. SENATOR FROM DELAWARE

Senator ROTH. Thank you, Mr. Chairman. I am pleased that you are holding this hearing today. Special 301 represents one of our most important trade tools in securing adequate and effective protection of U.S. intellectual property and obtaining market access for persons who rely on intellectual property in the global marketplace.

I am sure that today's testimony will underscore this fundamental point, particularly with respect to the upcoming June 30 Special 301 decision on China, India, and Argentina.

In addition to Special 301, the recent Uruguay Round Agreement on trade-related intellectual property rights, the so-called TRIPS Agreement, is a significant achievement in establishing multilateral standards of intellectual property protection.

But it represents a base line of protection on which to build higher levels of protection. There are, moreover, some special problems in the TRIPS agreement, particularly with respect to the long transition period that are provided to developing countries.

We are now faced with a situation where our country may be implementing an agreement by not implementing it for up to 10 years. The vigorous pursuit of strong international protection of intellectual property is a long-standing and well-established trade policy objective of the United States.

With the recent conclusion of the TRIPS Agreement, we must now establish a post-Uruguay Round strategy on intellectual property protection. Key elements of such a strategy must include monitoring the new TRIPS agreement to ensure that it is being adhered to as well as encouraging developing countries to accelerate their adoption of the TRIPS provision.

We must also continue our pursuit of more effective protection where necessary to bilateral, regional and multilateral approaches. Special 301 will continue to play an integral part of the post-Uruguay Round strategy.

I recently introduced legislation laying out such a strategy and I intend to work towards its inclusion in the Uruguay Round implementing legislation. I am pleased that the Chairman and Senator Danforth have also endorsed important aspects of this strategy. I look forward to working with both of them to ensure this critical issue is adequately addressed in the Uruguay Round bill.

Mr. Chairman, I would ask, since I will not be able to stay for the full hearing, that written questions be submitted.

Senator BAUCUS. Thank you very much, Senator, and they will be included.

[The questions appear in the appendix.]

Senator BAUCUS. Thank you for that statement.

I would now like to turn to our witnesses. Mr. Harvey Bale, who is a Senior Vice President for the International Division of the Pharmaceutical Research and Manufacturers of America; Mr. Jason Berman, Chairman and Chief Executive Officer of Recording Industry Association of America; and Mr. Robert Holleyman, President, Business Software Alliance.

Gentlemen, your full statements will automatically be included in the record. I urge you to summarize. I will not put a clock on you, but in return I urge you to be succinct, pithy, direct and to the point. Thank you.

Why do you not proceed, Dr. Bale?

STATEMENT OF HARVEY E. BALE, JR., PH.D., SENIOR VICE PRESIDENT, INTERNATIONAL DIVISION, PHARMACEUTICAL RESEARCH AND MANUFACTURERS OF AMERICA, WASHINGTON, DC

Dr. BALE. Thank you very much, Mr. Chairman. As you mentioned, I am Harvey Bale, Senior Vice President of Pharmaceutical Research and Manufacturers of America (PhRMA) and represent more than 100 research-based pharmaceutical companies, including 40 of the leading biotechnology companies.

PhRMA really does appreciate the support that has been given in a bipartisan way in both Congress and the administration, helping to ensure that the international trade environment becomes more conducive to the sale of innovative medicines derived from the research-based industry and as well for high-technology products in general.

These hearings, in deed, as you have mentioned, both gentlemen have mentioned, these hearings on Special 301 are taking place at a very important time for our industry and for the United States as a whole. We also understand, of course, that Congress is considering utilization of two other important trade instruments—free trade agreements and authority that goes with it, as well as the ratification of the GATT/Uruguay Round.

Special 301 has been and remains and should remain a key instrument in the range of trade tools that can be effective in convincing America's major trading partners to improve their respective intellectual property regimes.

Section and Special 301 have earned a special degree of importance because they have also helped to drive the progress and measured success that has occurred in the GATT.

From the perspective of the research-based pharmaceutical industry, the results of 301 actions included not only improved patent protection for pharmaceuticals in a number of countries, as you mentioned, Mr. Chairman, but has also led to, at a later point, in the establishment of the Special 301 procedure and the Trade Act of 1988; and these two together have both, as I just mentioned, led to, in fact, the successful Uruguay Round without the actions that would have been taken under those two provisions of law.

It is really quite doubtful that the progress that has been achieved in the GATT would have been achieved at all without Special 301. So I think the main point of this in our view is that not only is there intrinsic merit in the Special 301 process; but without a bilateral American strategy there can really be no multilateral system that advances and makes progress over the existing system.

As the Congress has begun to consider the Uruguay Round Agreement, we note there have been several pieces of legislation in tradition in Congress which attempt to deal with the critical flaws and the TRIPS Agreement, particularly the 10-year delayed implementation and lack of pipeline protection for pharmaceuticals and chemicals that injure the research-based industries in these areas.

In the Senate, as Senator Roth has mentioned, S.2173, the Intellectual Property Rights Protection Act of 1994 which contains many positive amendments to Special 301 and other U.S. trade statutes for the purpose of putting a halt to the theft of U.S. inventions.

PhRMA encourages such legislative initiatives insofar as they can provide considerable and positive incentives to foreign countries to improve their intellectual property regimes. We believe that this legislation does so.

Furthermore, PhRMA hardly endorses the proposed provisions relating to Section and Special 301 contained in the communication of June 22 from Committee Chairman Baucus and Senator Danforth. These provisions are essential, we believe, to a successful post-Uruguay Round trade strategy for America and would, if vigorously implemented, repair much of the harmful discrimination contained in the GATT TRIPS Agreement.

With respect to the issues that are at hand today with regard to decisions that must be made under the Special 301 procedure, Ambassador Kantor identified 37 trading partners that deny adequate and effective protection of IP or deny fair and equitable market access to U.S. persons that rely on intellectual property protection.

You further indicated that three of these trading partners—Argentina, China and India—pose the most significant problems in this area. Our Association member companies would support identification of the countries—India and Argentina—identified by USTR for such designation.

Indeed, in the case of India there is no other country in the world which has played a more insidious and damaging role for such a long period of time in terms of its total disregard for the norms of intellectual property protection, especially for pharmaceutical patents.

In Argentina we are still awaiting the results of a consideration of a draft patent law that was reintroduced in the Argentine Senate in 1993. And, indeed, the promises the Argentine Government made go back as far as 1989.

Mentioning also another country, Brazil, the Brazilian Government made a commitment to improve an existing patent law by adding amendments which reportedly would even exceed the provisions of the GATT TRIPS text. During the past five months these amendments have stalled and there have been no changes in the patent bill at all.

We understand now that there are no expectations that there will be any progress in the intellectual property area before the Brazilian elections this October. If this is the case, it would represent a broken commitment to the U.S. Government by the Brazilian Government once again. We would appreciate strong USTR action to designate Brazil as a priority foreign country or to take stronger action.

I should also mention Turkey in passing here, which has also promised to enact adequate patent legislation. We urge continued pressure where there at least has been some sign of progress that they are moving. However, again, their delayed implementation remains a problem.

We would also ask USTR to maintain China as a significant target of concern and action in the event that it does not fully live up to its commitments under the U.S.-China memorandum of understanding of January 1992.

In closing, Mr. Chairman, PhRMA looks forward to the opportunity to work closely with the Congress and the administration on the Uruguay Round implementing legislation, to ensure that in fact the intent of Congress in passing Special 301 1988 is carried forward in its implementation.

Thank you very much. We would appreciate any questions that may come later.

Senator BAUCUS. Thank you, Dr. Bale. We will have some questions later.

[The prepared statement of Dr. Bale with responses to questions submitted by Senator Roth and Senator Grassley appear in the appendix.]

Mr. Berman?

STATEMENT OF JASON S. BERMAN, CHAIRMAN AND CHIEF EXECUTIVE OFFICER, RECORDING INDUSTRY ASSOCIATION OF AMERICA, INC., WASHINGTON, DC

Mr. BERMAN. Thank you, Mr. Chairman. Let me begin by thanking you for inviting me, but more importantly for your initiative and interest in holding this hearing in the first place. Over the years the Trade Subcommittee's continued resolve in addressing the piracy of U.S. intellectual property in overseas markets has sent a message to our trading partners that piracy of U.S. works will be subject to trade retaliation.

Special 301 has indeed been of special importance in raising awareness around the world of the need to adequately and effectively protect intellectual property. Congressional enactment of this tool in the Trade Act of 1988 and its forceful and imaginative use by USTR has led to dramatic growth in the foreign sales of U.S. copyrighted materials.

While enforcement problems remain in many of the Pacific Rim countries, Special 301 has been used effectively in Japan, Korea, Taiwan and hopefully we can soon add to that Thailand.

Developments in intellectual property protection around the world, sparked by determined U.S. bilateral initiatives under Special 301 has led us to a new binding international discipline within the framework of the GATT, so-called TRIPS.

TRIPS, while incomplete, creates a new international benchmark for the protection and enforcement of intellectual property, and thus offers us a new launching pad for continued U.S. bilateralism to promote even more effective IP protection.

Negotiations over a TRIPS Agreement, for example, did not prevent or hamper our efforts to provide even stronger intellectual property protection in the NAFTA. TRIPS may resolve some questions, such as the rental of sound recordings and computer software and the term of copyright protection.

However, it either fails to address or does so only incompletely certain other questions, two of which are of central importance—market access for copyright based industries and questions related to the electronic transmission of works through global telecommunication systems.

The ability of the United States to continue to have a capacity to improve market conditions around the world in a post-Uruguay Round is dependent on the tools Congress fashions in GATT implementing legislation.

First, USTR must have clear and broad authority to take both trade and non-trade measures in response to the denial of adequate and effective intellectual property protection. This involves providing USTR greater discretion to take any action to respond to 301 violations and must make clear that the test of adequate and effective protection under Special 301 is not limited to the obligations contained in TRIPS.

Second, we must strengthen the trade tools that remain unaffected by the Uruguay Round and can serve as important points of leverage in securing improved protection in the future. I am referring in particular to GSP, to CBI and other trade programs.

In this regard, GSP should be renewed, as it provides perhaps the greatest single trade remedy available to secure improved intellectual property protection. Along these lines Special 301 should be modified to permit USTR to remove country eligibility totally pursuant to a Special 301 determination that a country has denied adequate and effective protection of intellectual property. This is a remedy already available under GSP and should be available under Special 301.

Third, Congress needs to work with the administration in fashioning an unambiguous set of negotiating objectives in the post-Uruguay Round environment. What remedies we can fashion to deal with intellectual property violations may have been affected by the GATT agreement. But what remains unaffected is our own decision making process about whether a practice unjustifiably, unfairly or unreasonable denies fair and equitable market access or where there is a lack of adequate and effective protection of intellectual property.

Fourth, Congress should move quickly to pass GATT implementing legislation, demonstrating our own commitment to the multilateral trading system and establishing a willingness on our part to maintain a leadership role within that system.

In implementing our GATT obligations, it is critical that we broadly interpret our obligations in certain key areas. The United States has traditionally done so in the copyright area. In particular, the U.S. must broadly construe Article 18 of the Berne Convention and restore protection to foreign works now in the public domain as was done for Mexico in NAFTA. Too frequently in the past our trading partners have cited our own narrow interpretation of the Berne Implementation Act to justify not protecting pre-existing U.S. works.

In addition, we need to enact a long overdue federal anti-bootleg statute.

U.S. performers and record companies have too frequently been denied protection because our trading partners have failed to take into account the protection available at the State level.

We have a great opportunity in GATT implementing legislation. It is the appropriate time to amend our own laws and we have a great deal to gain as the world's largest exporter of recorded music and other copyrighted works.

In closing, I just want to add one note about an important event in the life of Special 301. that is the question of designation by June 30. As you are well aware, USTR must decide by June 30 if China, Argentina and India are denying adequate and effective protection within the meaning of Special 301.

In announcing postponement of his decision in April, Ambassador Kantor noted that China and others would be designated, if solutions to the problems that had been identified were not reached. From my perspective, a solution means that China's 26 CD plants are no longer producing pirate CDs, either for local consumption or export, and that the Chinese have demonstrated their willingness and ability to fight piracy.

In the absence of meeting these conditions, and I do not believe they have been met to date, it is critical that China be identified on June 30. I urge you to communicate to the administration your support of that position.

Thank you, Mr. Chairman.

Senator BAUCUS. Thank you, Mr. Berman.

[The prepared statement of Mr. Berman with responses to questions submitted by Senator Grassley appears in the appendix.]

Senator BAUCUS. Mr. Holleyman?

STATEMENT OF ROBERT W. HOLLEYMAN II, PRESIDENT, BUSINESS SOFTWARE ALLIANCE, WASHINGTON, DC

Mr. HOLLEYMAN. Thank you, Mr. Chairman. I appreciate the opportunity to talk with you today about the concerns of the computer software industry with respect to the problem of piracy of U.S. computer programs outside of the United States.

The BSA represents the leading publishers of software for personal computers, companies like Aldus, Novell, WordPerfect, Microsoft and others.

Collectively our companies derive more than 50 percent of their annual revenues from foreign sales. So the problem of piracy of computer programs and ineffective protection abroad hits us directly. It also hits U.S. companies greatly because U.S. software companies have an estimated 74 percent of the world market for packaged software. Therefore not only are foreign revenues important to our companies, but our companies' foreign sales are important to the U.S. economy as a whole.

There are two issues which are under consideration today and I would like to add a third. The first issue deals with the implementation of the Special 301 provisions in the most recent Uruguay Round, looking particularly at the decisions that will be made with regard to China at the end of this month.

Second is the consideration of the implementation of Special 301 and additional trade mechanisms to protect intellectual property in light of the new WTO and the Uruguay Round.

The third issue I would like to add is an example of a sound confluence of U.S. trade policy involving the Hill, the administration and Special 301, where there have been very positive results for the software industry. That is a recent action in Japan.

On the first question, I can say that the United States was given an opportunity, in April, to designate countries that fail to protect intellectual property among our leading trade partners. The BSA recommended at that time—with our colleagues in the copyright community—that 28 countries be designated under the priority Foreign Country, Priority Watch List and Watch List categories.

For computer programs, in the 28 countries that we recommended, our losses for U.S. publishers alone totaled $2.8 billion in 1993. We would like to say that with one notable exception, the deferral of the decision on priority foreign countries, the BSA was generally pleased with the decisions that Ambassador Kantor announced on April 30.

All of the countries that we recommended for listing were, in fact, listed with only a couple of minor exceptions. However, the major exception for us, which I would like to address, is China.

Piracy of computer programs in China is rampant. The BSA has estimated that in 1993 94 percent of all software being used in China was pirated. For purposes of Special 301 we estimated that U.S. publishers alone lost $322 million, in 1993, in China because of the high rate of software piracy.

Overall, foreign software publishers and the local distribution chanel also suffered losses, which when combined with losses to U.S. publishers total $600 million in 1993. We have identified a series of major shortcomings in the Chinese law, and in the Chinese enforcement of their law, that we believe need to be rectified. These shortcomings are the reasons BSA recommended earlier this year, and continue to recommend today, designation of China as a priority foreign country.

For us these shortcomings are three-fold. The first is that there needs to be a criminal remedy, criminal penalties against copyright infringement in China. There is no other country that I am familiar with which has achieved noticeable reductions in piracy without having criminal penalties in addition to civil penalties. China must proceed with adoption of a criminal law.

Second, enforcement procedures in China must be improved. The Business Software Alliance filed, in March of this year, our first cases in China designed to bring and carry out raids against software retail stores and computer hardware dealers that were selling pirated goods.

The evidence we had was voluminous. It was clear. It was not with question. We filed our cases at the beginning of March. The cases dragged on and on. We were asked to file more papers. We were asked to increase the fees that we had paid to the courts. It was truly one of the most difficult enforcement encounters that we have experienced in any country of the more than 50 in which we do anti-piracy work.

I am pleased, however, to report that only yesterday, and finally yesterday, did we get our raids carried out. Five successful raids against software dealers and hardware dealers in and around Beijing were completed. We seized at that time, more than 300 programs which were copied and pirated, as well as hardware that was being used for duplication.

Our early reports indicate that the raids proceeded just as we had hoped, but it did not proceed as we had hoped in March. I think that it is no coincidence that these raids were executed on the eve of the June 30 decision on priority foreign country status.

We are pleased that the raids were carried out. We are completely dissatisfied with the process that it took to get us from there to where we are today. So, we continue to believe that designation of China, on June 30, is required as a means of ensuring that the Chinese Government continues to fulfill their commitments to enforcement which they made, in 1992, as part of the memorandum of understanding.

Finally, I would like to add that what we have seen in this recent process is that there is no transparency in the Chinese process for bringing cases. It is a byzantine requirement. It is not laid out so that copyright owners can easily avail themselves of the process. And, in fact, we believe that it was suggested we try alternative mechanisms which would, in our view, completely eliminate any rule of law that should be in place in China.

Therefore, it is our view that the combination of the absence of criminal penalties, the delays of enforcement, and the absence of transparency, in the process, all require a designation of China on June 30.

In terms of our requirements under the WTO, the BSA and the software industry strongly support adoption of the Uruguay Round and adoption of the implementing legislation by this Congress. The TRIPS provisions, in the Round, will for the first time provide a multilateral basis on copyright protection for software as a literary work with a 50-year term and a software rental provision.

All of which are provisions we have sought in our bilateral trade agreements over the past decade. We strongly support passage of the implementing legislation by this Congress. It is in the best interest of the software industry.

With that in mind, we believe it is also important, as my colleagues have testified, to look at alternative mechanisms that can be used to supplement what remains of our enforcement ability under Special 301. We favor looking at using GSP, the CBI, bank guarantees, and loans, any mechanism that can supplement the Special 301 provisions.

But taken as a whole, we believe there will be a major step forward for the U.S. if, in fact, the requirements of the TRIPS agreement are imposed through the new World Trade Organization.

Finally, let me just conclude with an example of where a Special 301 and effective trade policy can work. I testified before this subcommittee in November, of this past year, about what was then a very eminent threat in Japan.

U.S. software companies have a 60 percent market share in Japan. We have achieved that through two reasons—one, by creating innovative programs; and, two, in 1984 the U.S. was successful in concluding a bilateral agreement with Japan to provide copyright protection for software.

Last summer the Japanese ministry of education announced a proposal to consider weakening the Japanese copyright law to allow the decompilation of computer programs. That would have directly hurt the ability of U.S. companies to do business in Japan; and had it been adopted as a model in other countries, it would have hurt the ability of U.S. software companies to do our business around the world.

When the study was announced, I first went to Tokyo, in October, to discuss it. We were told that U.S. companies were not invited to participate in the process; and that while we might comment informally, we were not to be allowed to participate in a formal capacity.

The U.S. Government, through this Congress, through the Senate,through your assistance, Mr. Chairman, as well as through the strong assistance at USTR, at the Commerce Department, and by Ambassador Mondale on the ground in Tokyo, went to work and identified the decompilation initiative as a matter of the gravest concern to the U.S. Government and to U.S. trade policy.

At the end of last month the study commission finally released its result. Much to our surprise, given that the leading elements of Japanese Federation of Industries, Keidanren, had advocated a gutting of the copyright law. The study commission came forward with their recommendation and their recommendation was to defer any further consideration of legislative changes in the Japanese copyright law in the area of decompilation of computer programs.

We view that as a very significant victory, although I might add an interim victory. But, it removed from the table at present what was an eminent threat to U.S. software companies doing business in Japan and it only happened because of the action of this Congress, because of the support of the administration, and also by the effective designation of Japan as a priority watch list country on April 30.

I think that shows that the confluence of trade policy and Special 301 does work. It can work. It is our hope that it will now work in the case of China and other Priority Foreign Countries.

Thank you very much.

Senator BAUCUS. Thank you very much, Mr. Holleyman.

[The prepared statement of Mr. Holleyman with responses to questions from Senators Hatch and Grassley appear in the appendix.]

Senator BAUCUS. I would like to ask each of you a general question. You have all somewhat commented on it, but I would like you to flesh it out in a little bit more detail.

That is, although each of your industries has a little bit different perspective on this, generally what you see the United States gains in intellectual property protection with the proposed TRIPS Agreement and the Uruguay Round, what we do not get, and how we deal with the difference.

Again, I know it is a bit different for each of your industries. I will start with you, Dr. Bale. I know you all advocated supporting the Round. But if you could just outline for this subcommittee why you believe your industry is better protected from the intellectual property point of view compared with not ratifying the Round, what we gain, and what we give up.

Then I am going to ask all of you questions of how we modify, if at all, Special 301 in light of what the result would be. Again, assuming that the United States does ratify the Round.

Dr. Bale?

Dr. BALE. Mr. Chairman, that is a very good question. The benefits to industries that are in the high technology manufacturing sector, such as pharmaceuticals—and I will try to generalize a little bit; we are perhaps the only industry represented here from the manufacturing side—would be taking many countries which, in fact, in the past have through their national laws protected by patent and by trademark and industrial trade secret protection, puts this into the form of an international agreement, which makes the level of obligation existent, which right now does not exist under Paris Conventions and various other conventions that are there on the books but they do not have any mechanism of enforcement.

So by providing for 20-year patent, basic patent, protection for pharmaceuticals, for example, by providing for trademark protection, by putting very strict limits on compulsory licensing, this really does go far to setting up an international regime that can be built upon.

Now those are the pluses. On the minuses, there are a number of questions that exist in the TRIPS agreement with regard to how it will be implemented. There are ambiguities. There are interpretations, for example, in Article 30 with regard to exceptions to rights under patents which maybe we may see trucks being driven through those exceptions. Those are going to be major issues in the future.

That makes it all the more serious, the delayed implementation, with regard to about 20 or 30 countries that right now do not protect pharmaceuticals by product patent protection.

In three markets alone—in Argentina, Brazil and in India—we lose about $1.5 billion in sales per year. So if you look at a 10-year implementation of those agreements, as the TRIPS Agreements, as now exists in the draft text, we are looking at a cost that is over $10 billion—$15 billion approximately, just multiplying it by 10—that really accounts for a lot of lost research capability of our companies and unfairly distributes the burden of spreading R&D to those countries that, in fact, do have a patent protection.

So basically our major concern is that the delayed implementation which was driven basically by one major developing country that for whatever reasons are historical and institutional, both within the GATT structure, and in the negotiating process—and that country is basically India, and has been at the core of delayed implementation, that is our major serious deficiency. That is where we will continue to lose billions of dollars over the next decade as a result of the TRIPS Agreement.

So that is the pluses and those are the minuses that we think are existing in the TRIPS Agreement.

Senator BAUCUS. As you know, Senator Danforth and I are suggesting implementing language which tends to accelerate—the time within which the USTR could at least put countries like India on a watch list or priority list or some way to deal with that 10-year delay.

If the United States ratifies the Round, how far do you think we can go under Special 301 having signed the agreement to move in that direction?

Dr. BALE. Well, I think we can do some of the things that my colleagues have mentioned to broaden the scope of action. I think that that is certainly suggested by your joint communication to Ambassador Kantor. I think there are a lot of thoughts that are being given to this.

Clearly, in signing an agreement that has a multilateral system that is put in place with these delays in no way excuses, I think, the administration and the government from pursuing other avenues, bilateral mechanisms, whether they be through free-trade agreements or through Special 301 or formal diplomatic channels.

Diplomatic channels will be rather empty in content without a good, strong Special 301 mechanism. Those should still exist. I see no inconsistency. In fact, if the United States is going to continue to be the leader for liberalized trade, as we have been—I mean, we cannot count on the European community, nor Japan, nor any of the countries that are in the GATT other than ourselves.

88-739 O - 95 - 2

I think it really behooves us to make sure that our own interests at the same time are not sacrificed to that multilateral system, because without these bilateral initiatives I frankly think the World Trade Organization is going to become the graveyard of trade liberalization, not its source of growth.

That bilateral initiative, coupled with the multilateral system that we have, I see no inconsistency whatsoever.

Senator BAUCUS. Would you suggest modification of Special 301?

Dr. BALE. I think what we have suggested, in fact, and is seen in some legislation, that is proposed both in the communication that you suggest to the administration and what Senator Roth has put forward, does look at expanded and perhaps extended use of such areas as GSP. Looking at the area of science and technology agreements, there is a vast array and I hope that over the next couple of weeks as the Congress begins to consider seriously the content of the administrative actions that the administration can take, and the marked up legislation that is put forward, some of these ideas can be gathered and put on the table.

Senator BAUCUS. What leverage do we have on India? You know, China exports a lot of products to the United States that we could retaliate against. India does not export nearly as much. What trade leverage do we have in India, for example?

Dr. BALE. Certainly the pressure of notoriety that is given to India as part of the Special 301 process is in and of itself a valued instrument. Clearly, India is being singled out here as one of the most notorious patent pirate countries and counterfeiting countries.

Senator BAUCUS. Does notoriety work with India?

Dr. BALE. Not enough. No, it is not enough. That is right.

Senator BAUCUS. That is my experience, it does not.

Dr. BALE. A couple of years ago GSP was an instrument that had been used by the administration and GSP was taken away to a considerable extent in the pharmaceutical and chemical area. There is still a fair amount of GSP left on the table. I think we need to use those instruments and see how far we can get.

There is a problem with regard to a country like India other than it does not exist in Argentina or Brazil and China, and that is that India exports only approximately 4 percent of its total gross national product in international commerce.

Yet we see that India does have a disproportionate influence in the WTO as it has had in the GATT. One of the Deputy Director Generals, for example, always seems to be a national of that country.

So I think it is an area that we will have to continue to work with the administration and the Congress on. I do believe GSP has some effect. I believe we have to go beyond it. India ultimately will be interested in joining the rest of the world with regard to science issues and learning about what is going on in the rest of the world and adopting some of it, some of those techniques.

And I think the United States ought to be very reluctant to devote the resources of organizations such as the White House Science Advisor, the Food and Drug Administration and the certification of Indian facilities for the shipment of products to the United States.

So over time I think the pressure and the notoriety of being singled out as an outlier country and the general progress toward intellectual property strengthening will have some effect. But unless we keep the pressure on through Special 301, then I think the absolute opposite will occur—total relaxation by the Indian Government. It will leave the pirates in India a clear day over the next decade or more. In fact, it will undermine ultimately the interpretation of the TRIPS Agreement.

One of the most damaging aspects of the delay in implementation of TRIPS that we see is that we simply will not see how Indian courts, how Brazilian and Argentinean courts for that matter, will actually interpret TRIPS in actual practice.

We are giving these guys a 10-year holiday—i.e., to even begin to think about getting down to rolling up their sleeves and working out a system of protection of chemicals and pharmaceuticals.

Senator BAUCUS. Some might argue that we have agreed to give a 10-year holiday if we ratify.

Dr. BALE. I think what we have agreed to is a broad package of issues in the Uruguay Round, some of which are a benefit and some of which need further work. I think that there is no inconsistency, nor have I heard any statements coming out of the Trade Representative that say other than the 5- to 10-year delayed implementation of TRIPS is nothing but an abomination and it needs to be rectified.

Senator BAUCUS. All right. Thank you.

Mr. Berman, generally.

Mr. BERMAN. After Harvey's answer, I forgot the question.

Senator BAUCUS. Well, the basic question is just——

Mr. BERMAN. I have it, Mr. Chairman.

In regard to the U.S. recording industry I would say the gains are represented by codification or the term of protection and the rental right, retroactivity for sound recordings, protection for U.S. performers and enforcement—all very critical areas. I would say these have been achieved principally as a result of 5 years of U.S. bilateral agreements based on Special 301s.

I think this point may have been made by Harvey. So what is represented in TRIPS is really in a way a codification of what the U.S. has sought to achieve through the instrument of Special 301. In that regard, it has been an enormously successful trade tool.

The failures are also, incredibly important. The most notable being the fact that the so-called cultural industries were forced to choose between an EC proposal that was a disaster and being left out of it completely. We chose voluntarily to be left out.

The other failures, therefore, result from that—a lack of national treatment, a lack of market access, and an inability to deal with the future of digital communications. So that what we have is a new base line embodied in TRIPS which does not remove the need for Special 301 to be modified in such a way that it takes into account the more limited remedies available by virtue of tariff bindings and other things; and to figure out how we can move forward in the future by reconfiguring Special 301.

It must remain an important ingredient in our arsenal. It can and it needs to be supplemented by the addition of non-trade measures into the equation. The United States by virtue of its own marketplace holds an enormous number of cards in regard to its trading partners. It needs to be willing to play those cards.

Senator BAUCUS. You make a very good point. I very much agree. I think that Special 301 has had that effect; and I think it has for several reasons. Number one, the United States, I think, does lead the world in intellectual property. That is clear. So we have a lot to gain and a lot to lose that is very important to the United States.

As you say, Mr. Berman, we are still the largest market. But even beyond that, I think one of the main benefits of Special 301 is it has deadlines. It has certain classifications—it has watch lists and regular and priority watch lists, named countries.

Mr. BERMAN. Let me point out in that regard, Mr. Chairman, I think the deadlines are an important ingredient and the deadlines by virtue of being set in the statute were critical.

What is also critical is to maintain the kind of discretionary authority that supplements the so-called deadlines. For example, there is only one designation statutorily under 301, priority foreign country. All of a sudden in the last few years we have had a variety of categories emerge as a result of USTR's, I would say, imaginative use of the tools available to it.

Now in some cases we benefited and in some cases we may not have benefited. But nevertheless, as a result of being able to embellish upon the statutory authority given in 1988, we have a totally different tool than the one that was necessarily enacted into law.

So I agree that the mandatory time table has been an essential feature, but I would urge also to think about the idea that lack of predictability is equally important, in trade negotiations in particular—I am reminded, for example, that very early in this administration the Wall Street Journal did a story about Ambassador Kantor and USTR, accusing the United States and USTR in particular of being unclear—the U.S. policy could not be read. It was here one day; here another day.

Senator BAUCUS. I remember that.

Mr. BERMAN. You remember that.

Senator BAUCUS. I remember that piece.

Mr. BERMAN. Mr. Chairman, as someone whose livelihood in some respects as Mr. Holleyman pointed out, is dependent upon foreign markets, well over 50 percent of the music we sell is sold outside the United States, I thought that was the greatest thing.

The idea that U.S. policy was a mystery to some people was an important negotiating ingredient and I think it has been in the context in which Special 301 has been implemented. So I would urge that we find a way to marry the important feature of mandatory deadlines with the ability to have flexibility in the negotiation.

I think the worst thing that could happen in the United States to regard to its trade policy in the post- Uruguay Round is to simply have it down here on a piece of paper.

Senator BAUCUS. I appreciate that. What is the recording industry and the motion picture association going to do now that you voluntarily opted out of this cultural matter?

Mr. BERMAN. Well, we voluntarily opted out of a very bad agreement. it is our hope that, one, we will make some improvements in U.S. law which would remove from the dialogue with our European friends the idea that somehow European law is superior to U.S. law and, therefore, there is no basis of coming to an agreement.

This has been an irritant in the U.S.-EC dialogue. it is our intention to continue to press forward in a dialogue with the Europeans.

Senator BAUCUS. What leverage are you going to use? What leverage do you have?

Mr. BERMAN. Well, that unfortunately is the issue in which we are hoping that the reconfiguration of Special 301 might give us something that we do not have in our armor today. It is very difficult at this moment to say what that would be.

Senator BAUCUS. Mr. Holleyman, your response to this general question, speaking with regard to the software industry?

Mr. HOLLEYMAN. Mr. Chairman, I think that Special 301 should be utilized to the fullest extent possible in the new environment by addressing issues that were not addressed in the Uruguay Round, such as elimination of other market barriers, national treatment issues, parallel import protection, items that were excluded in their entirety from the agreement.

Second, I emphasize again the point I think most of us have made that there are other mechanisms, like GSP, CBI, bank loans that can creatively be used.

Senator BAUCUS. When you say bank loans, which loans are you referring to?

Mr. HOLLEYMAN. I think any U.S.—either by the U.S. exercising its right as a voting member of any of the international institutions we can. For example, I think this is creative but it is something we have been working on for some time. Many of the multilateral banks of which the U.S. owns a majority of shares or has a key role extend loans to developing countries to purchase computer hardware.

Many of those countries purchase the hardware but never purchase the software. They simply pirate the software. I think it would be very easy for the U.S. to recognize, through its voting membership in those organizations, that a simple part of the extension of loans is an examination of the purpose for which the loan is being extended.

If it is a sizeable loan for the purchase of computer hardware, it should be accompanied with a requirement for the purchase of software as well, because the hardware absent the software does nothing. It is a problem we have identified and we have been working on for some months now. I think that is just one example of what the U.S. could do.

But taken as a whole, I cannot emphasize strongly enough just how much the software industry supports the agreement that was reached and the TRIPS requirement. We think that by extending a protection of software under copyright on a multilateral basis in conjunction with the remaining mechanism that the U.S. has under 301 and through the extension of other mechanisms will be a win-win situation for the software industry and, indeed, for the U.S. economy.

So we fully support passage of the implementing legislation at the earliest possible time.

Senator BAUCUS. Last year I think you told us in written testimony that Singapore still refuses to take actions even against large scale counterfeit operations. I think that was your quote. Is that still continuing?

Mr. HOLLEYMAN. They have begun to take actions against large scale counterfeit operations.

Senator BAUCUS. Who is the Michael Fay of the Singapore counterfeiters?

Mr. HOLLEYMAN. Well, the Michael Fay was a gentleman named Mr. Ong, from 2 years ago, who was using Singapore as an assembly point for packaging computer software that was being shipped around the world. That was a case that we had originally brought to the attention of the Singapore Government. They did nothing about it.

Senator BAUCUS. What are the penalties for counterfeiting compared with vandalism? I am just curious what it might be.

Mr. HOLLEYMAN. The legal penalties are actually fairly good. To the best of my knowledge, they do not involve caning, but there are substantial penalties in Singapore. The problem we had there was that the government was doing absolutely nothing to enforce it. They were simply——

Senator BAUCUS. Which means Singapore now is enforcing?

Mr. HOLLEYMAN. Singapore has begun within the past six months to eight months to carry out selected enforcement actions. We do not think it is enough, but they have stated.

Senator BAUCUS. Dr. Bale?

Dr. BALE. I can intervene on that. Since you raised Singapore, there is another potential issue in TRIPS that we hope the Congress and administration will watch very carefully. Between now and the time the TRIPS or the World Trade Organization is actually implemented, and we hope it is January 1, 1995, countries are free to retrogress in their level of treatment of intellectual property.

In fact, in Singapore we have seen very recently the government start to reintroduce notions of compulsory licensing which the rest of the world has been abandoning. So there is another problem in the TRIPS area, which is again requiring almost a mandatory element for the U.S. to have a Special 301 to deal with it. Because if we do not have an active vigorous bilateral program, we may not necessarily even have the rules to prevent countries from taking advantage of a gap or window of opportunity to deny intellectual property protection to U.S. works.

Senator BAUCUS. I would like to go back to the question of deadlines. How important are deadlines in Special 301? Mr. Berman, you mentioned they are good. But it is also good to be creative and be a little bit unpredictable and so forth.

Do you have any worries of deadlines slipping. The April 30 deadline slipped. I mean apparently at least in one case-China-for foreign policy reasons. Does that concern you?

Mr. BERMAN. Foreign policy concerns have always interceded in trade issues in the formulation of U.S. policy. I cannot say we were surprised by the postponement this time in regard to China. It got a little more complicated by MFN.

It is an essential ingredient that there be time tables. I think the greatest worry in the case of China in the postponement was the fact that it was a very confusing signal. It could easily have been read by the Chinese in such a way that were the United States to make a decision, which I hope it would, on June 30 to designate China as a priority foreign country that the Chinese could have felt, my God, you know, this is a turnabout in policy.

You postponed it. You know, you gave us some more time. We have been talking. How can you name us now? I think that is the danger it seems to me. So it sometimes works to your advantage and sometimes it works to your disadvantage.

I believe in the time tables I would like to see it fashioned in such a way that certainly in crafting the remedies there is enough room for discretion.

Senator BAUCUS. Frankly, I would err more on the side of sticking to the time tables. I mean, because then countries know what to expect and then, you know, those kinds of matters are not added to the calculation. It automatically has happened and is expected and so forth. I frankly do not know what is gained, by delay, particularly when as you say too often trade policy is handmade in foreign policy.

If we are to elevate and continue to elevate, which I think is important, economic and trade matters, to me, that argues a little more towards sticking with the time tables. But there is a difference of opinion.

Dr. Bale?

Dr. BALE. Mr. Chairman, the only real justification there can be for letting a time table slip is if a country is demonstrating such significant progress and its own internal clockwork—its legislative, its administrative procedures—might prevent the time table from coinciding with the time that is necessary to actually implement it. I think only in that circumstance can one really begin to justify a delay.

We are reminded of the recent events regarding Brazil wherein the case of that country there had been some understandings between the U.S. Government and Brazil about a time table which, in fact, the Brazilian Government itself had set for itself in enacting legislation protecting pharmaceutical products, which was June 15. That time has come and gone and absolutely nothing has happened.

So here it is very difficult then to justify anything but strong action in response to an issue that has been dragging itself out since President Collor first became President of Brazil back in 1989.

Senator BAUCUS. What is your view on the waiver question, the GATT waiver? I mean, do you have a view on that, the three of you, on how important it is for the United States to raise the revenues $14 billion or whatever it is or waive?

Dr. BALE. It is pretty tough to argue that somehow in a process of trade liberalization for the purposes of freeing up trade and eliminating trade barriers and creating an opportunity to generate economic growth and ultimately to recoup those revenues to look for a static analysis of what is essentially a very dynamic benefit to the U.S. economy.

In our field of intellectual property—the industries represented here—dynamism is competition. I mean, without basically the intellectual property field you make no progress whatsoever. Therefore, you have to look at this in the long-term environment.

So for us looking at this issue of trying to recoup revenues based upon a very static analysis, that we understand is mandated, is to us a very ironic and unfortunately counter productive exercise. Because you may wind up destroying some of the incentive that is created by the basic round. But, of course, this is an issue which we in the private sector are watching with some horror and amazement and waiting for the decisions to come from the administration and Congress about where the axe may fall.

Senator BAUCUS. Thank you.

Mr. Berman?

Mr. BERMAN. I guess it depends on where the axe falls. Generally speaking, I think as a matter of public policy, the waiver makes sense in an instance like this. How does Congress go about doing that is a much more complicated political question and legislative question.

But I do believe that in general on an issue of this sort that a general waiver would be appropriate.

Senator BAUCUS. Mr. Holleyman?

Mr. HOLLEYMAN. The software industry grew by 269 percent over the 1982 to 1992 period, compared to the rest of the U.S. economy which grew by 30 percent during that same time. If this, coupled with the foreign sales by U.S. companies is any indication, liberalizing trade opportunities, as well as providing for protection of U.S. software sold abroad should redound enormously to the benefit of the growth of the U.S. economy, which I would argue that that weighs in favor of waving the Budget Act requirements.

Senator BAUCUS. So your industries are not going to be all upset if we are not "reducing the budget deficit," that we are abdicating our responsibility if we waive? I mean, some people in business get a little upset when Congress takes action that is perceived as increasing the deficit as opposed to reducing the deficit.

Dr. BALE. I do not think we believe, Mr. Chairman, we are really increasing the deficit. We understand the calculus of the issue and I know that also presents congress with very difficult political issues. But I guess our philosophy would be that there is not a net increment in the deficit in the long term.

Senator BAUCUS. All right. I have no more questions to ask. I just want to follow-up by saying that I very much hope the administration on June 30 lives up to its responsibilities and names the countries that we have indicated here.

Second, I urge you and others who are interested,and I know there are others interested in working with us in developing an add-on or amendment to Special 301 and related statutes so that we can continue to be the primary engine in free trade and protection of intellectual property.

You have made some good suggestions and I think it is important we follow-up on them so that we can take best advantage of them. Beyond that, has anybody said anything so outrageous that it deserves an answer?

[No audible response.]

Senator BAUCUS. Thank you very much for your testimony. The hearing is adjourned.

[Whereupon, at 3:11 p.m., the hearing was adjourned.]

APPENDIX

ADDITIONAL MATERIAL SUBMITTED

PREPARED STATEMENT OF HARVEY E. BALE, JR.

Mr. Chairman and Members of the Subcommittee: I am Harvey E. Bale, Senior Vice President of the Pharmaceutical Research and Manufacturers of America. PhRMA—formerly the Pharmaceutical Manufacturers Association—represents more than 100 research-based pharmaceutical companies, including more than 40 of the country's leading biotechnology companies. PhRMA members discover, develop and produce most of the prescription drugs used in the United States and a substantial portion of the medicines used abroad.

I appreciate the opportunity to appear today at this important hearing on the Special 301 trade remedy law and its vital importance to the research-based pharmaceutical industry as a means to improve intellectual property protection around the world.

PhRMA appreciates the decade-long bipartisan support in both the Congress and the Executive Branch, in helping to ensure that the international trade environment becomes more conducive to the sale of innovative medicines derived from the research-based pharmaceutical industry, as well as U.S. products in general.

These hearings on Special 301 are taking place at a very important time both for our industry and for the United States, as the Congress also is considering the utilization of two other important trade instruments: These are the negotiation of Free Trade Agreements (FTAs), especially with countries in the Western Hemisphere as a follow-on to the successful conclusion of the plurilateral North American Free Trade Agreement (NAFTA), and the ratification of the multilateral GATT Uruguay Round Agreement. Both contain provisions on Trade-Related Intellectual Property issues (TRIPs) which are of significant interest to the research-based pharmaceutical industry; however, the transition in the latter is of particular concern, and I will speak to this later in greater detail.

Special 301 is a key instrument in the range of trade tools that can be effective in convincing America's major trading partners to improve their respective intellectual property regimes.

Section and Special 301 have earned a special degree of importance because they have served to drive progress and measured success in the GATT. FTAs also can play an important role in improving intellectual property protection, but these are individual agreements which must be negotiated on a country-by-country basis, and which may or may not be driven by negotiations under Special 301. Special 301, moreover, is viewed by many governments as the standard against which they measure America's interest in the intellectual property issue.

There have been instances in this country's recent trade history when an apparent over-reliance on multilateral trade mechanisms has eroded the domestic support base for a national trade policy especially within the private sector. Such was the case in September 1985, when a private sector advisory group released a report that was highly critical of the GATT-focus in the policy of the Administration at that time. That report helped convince the Executive Branch to launch a series of self-initiated bilateral investigations involving services, market access issues and intellectual property practices.

From the perspective of the research-based pharmaceutical industry, the results of 301 actions included not only improved patent protection for pharmaceuticals in a number of countries, but also the establishment of the "Special 301" provision in the Trade Act of 1988. This also led to the successful inclusion of intellectual property issues in GATT negotiations within the Uruguay Round which began in 1986.

The successful conclusion of the Uruguay Round and the signing of the GATT text in April doubtlessly provide the U.S. another trade instrument to improve global intellectual property protection. While PhRMA supports prompt Congressional implementation of the Uruguay Round, we do so on the understanding that the U.S. Government vigorously will continue bilateral efforts to improve intellectual property protection in patent-infringing countries, and that we forthrightly address the transition period which remains unacceptable.

It is extremely regrettable that the United States was not able to eliminate the discriminatory aspects of TRIPs in the final agreement. This includes the fact that some signatories will be allowed an inordinately long time to implement the TRIPs provisions. Moreover, the TRIPs text contains no pipeline provisions to grant protection to qualifying products that have been patented outside of but not yet marketed within signatory countries. Nonetheless, the United States still may avail itself of several policy options to continue to protect U.S. inventions from patent piracy before TRIPs is implemented.

Our industry believes, for example, that Special 301 and the trade measures that we may utilize under Special 301, including the Generalized System of Preferences (GSP), must be used to encourage developing countries to implement patent protection for pharmaceutical products, especially during the period of the overly long and discriminatory delay—in some cases, up to ten years of delay—allowed for certain signatories in Article 65 of the GATT TRIPs agreement.

If we move too far down the road Of multilateral trade diplomacy without maintaining access to bilateral trade mechanisms, all of us who support free trade in this country risk losing the support of the American public for our important trade objectives. Indeed, the World Trade Organization (WTO), which is the world body envisioned by the GATT Agreement, to be responsible for the adjudication and resolution of international trade disputes, could become a veritable "graveyard" of free trade without an aggressive U.S. posture in the bilateral area.

Our goal also is to convince nations, such as India, Argentina, Brazil and Turkey which represent the last bastions of global patent piracy, that to adopt effective patent protection for pharmaceutical products is in their best economic and trade interests.

Indeed, in the next few days, the Administration will be making a very critical decision on the Special 301 status for India. We believe it is necessary that a strong message be sent to India, since it remains one of the bastions of global piracy, not only in the country itself, but as exporters. Additionally, India is known to have been the leader in the GATT, arguing for the long transition period and no pipeline. The U.S. must, in other words, keep India at the most demanding priority level if we are to remain credible towards India as well to a host of other countries which will be watching closely.

We also should take comfort in the fact that such a stance will not only be beneficial to America economically, but will benefit Indians, because a good Indian patent law will lead to higher quality medicine for Indians, and overall better healthcare in that country. We need only point to the most noteworthy successes of Special 301-related trade negotiations, including those with the Andean Pact, China, Hungary, Indonesia, the Philippines, Taiwan and Thailand to demonstrate the effectiveness of this bilateral mechanism, and that these countries are benefitting economically as well as in terms of quality of their healthcare.

Mr. Chairman, you and other members of this Committee have served as exemplary leaders in the epic struggle against global patent piracy. We have appreciated your efforts in this regard and look forward to working with you and this important Subcommittee on International Trade in the months and years ahead.

CONSIDERATION OF CONGRESSIONAL LEGISLATION AFFECTING INTELLECTUAL PROPERTY PROTECTION

As the Congress has begun consideration of the Uruguay Round Agreement, we note that there have been several pieces of legislation introduced in the Congress which attempt to deal with those critical flaws in the TRIPs agreement, i.e., the 10 year delayed implementation and lack of pipeline protection for pharmaceuticals, that injure the research-based pharmaceutical industry.

In the Senate, in particular, on June 9, Senator Roth introduced S. 2173, the Intellectual Property Rights Protection Act of 1994, which also contains many positive amendments to Special 301 and other U.S. trade statutes for the purpose of putting a halt to the theft of U.S. inventions. PhRMA encourages such legislative initiatives insofar as they can provide considerable and positive incentives to foreign countries to improve their intellectual property regimes.

Furthermore, PhRMA heartily endorses the proposed provisions relating to Section 301 and Special 301 contained in the communication of June 22 from Committee Chairman Baucus and Senator Danforth. These provisions are essential to a successful post-Uruguay Round trade strategy for America, and would, if vigorously implemented, repair much of the harmful discrimination contained in the GATT TRIPs agreement.

THE IMPORTANCE OF INTELLECTUAL PROPERTY PROTECTION

Pharmaceutical breakthroughs, including those from biotechnology, provide the best and most cost-effective hope for new cures and treatments for life-threatening and debilitating diseases. The rise of biotechnology follows earlier scientific advances that also led to better understanding of disease and ultimately more effective medicines. Products now in the pipeline could provide more cures and better controls for many of today's most intractable and costly diseases. This research is costly, averaging $359 million for each new product, according to government estimates.

It is a fact that while research into new medicines is extremely costly, many medicines can be copied at a small fraction of their development cost. We are, therefore, understandably concerned about the ten years of delay granted to developing countries before they must implement TRIPs and the lack of pipeline protection. Taken together, these mean that the GATT will not yield adequate and effective protection of pharmaceutical patents in many countries for more than a decade. These countries include those designated this past year under Special 301 as Priority Foreign Country, such as Argentina and India or as Priority Watch Country, such as Turkey, or identified as "having continuing or prospective problems," such as Brazil.

INTELLECTUAL PROPERTY PROTECTION IN TRIPS

The GATT TRIPs text is a substantial step forward as a multilateral trade agreement. However, the world has changed considerably since the Uruguay Round negotiations began in 1986. There has been a growing recognition of the importance of intellectual property protection to high-technology manufacturing industries such as the pharmaceutical, and its related biotechnology, industry.

Tens of thousands of high-technology pharmaceutical jobs depend on strong worldwide intellectual property protection. Bilateral intellectual property agreements, as well as NAFTA, have been negotiated with many countries from Eastern Europe to Latin America to China that represent significant advances over the TRIPs text in several areas, most notably in the timing of the application of new intellectual property protection.

Regrettably, TRIPs allows for a ten year delay in patent protection and does not provide immediate "pipeline" protection to qualifying products whose patents have been granted outside of signatory countries, but not yet marketed in those countries at the time the law goes into effect. This means that it will not benefit the international research-based pharmaceutical industry significantly in many rapidly growing markets in Asia, Africa and Latin America until at least 2005. It also means that these governments regrettably can deny their citizens the benefits of first-rate pharmaceutical patents.

I also would note that the ten year delayed implementation period in TRIPs includes an extra five years of delay which discriminates against pharmaceuticals. For most areas of technology, developing countries have five years in which to conform to the TRIPs obligations. However, to the extent that countries do not protect pharmaceutical product patents, they have an extra five years to conform to TRIPs, and, in many instances, an extra five years to pirate U.S. inventions. It is regrettable that the United States agreed to a result which discriminates against one of its most competitive high-technology manufacturing industries.

Patent piracy, however, affects not only the ability of the industry to support the costly innovation necessary to discover new medicines, but there is compelling evidence that piracy also endangers the public health in developing countries.

In January 1992, the British journal *Nature* reported that much of the trade in counterfeit drugs-which is reaching epidemic proportions in places such as Brazil and Nigeria- originates "from developing countries that do not recognize the patents owned by multinational drug companies." Clearly, in countries such as Bangladesh, India and Nigeria, the lack of protection for intellectual property adds to an environment where lack of regulation and enforcement of pharmaceutical regulations allows dangerous counterfeiting to flourish.

Another key area in which the TRIPs agreement does not offer adequate intellectual property protection is in the vital biotechnology field. TRIPs Article 27.3 would allow GATT signatories to exclude from patentability plant and animal varieties other than microorganisms, an exclusion which could have significant adverse effects on biotechnology-derived products.

Biotechnology is another area where the U.S. industry is the world leader. Of the 167 biotechnology patents for genetically engineered pharmaceuticals/health care products granted in 1993, 146 went to Americans. .

U.S. TRADE POLICY AND INTELLECTUAL PROPERTY PROTECTION

These flaws in TRIPs stand in marked contrast to the progress toward better intellectual property protection for pharmaceuticals achieved by U.S. negotiators in NAFTA and in many bilateral negotiations conducted under the authority of the Section 301 and, in particular, the Special 301 provision of U.S. trade law. PhRMA strongly believes that, given the undue, costly and counterproductive delay in effective application of the TRIPs text, the United States should accelerate rather than slacken its bilateral efforts.

Since the enactment of the Trade and Tariff Act of 1984, intellectual property infringement has been defined as an unfair trade practice. Both the Congress and the Executive Branch have supported vigorous enforcement of Section 301 to enforce intellectual property rights abroad. It is largely as a result of this consistent U.S. policy that intellectual property rights are included—for the first time—in a GATT agreement.

The willingness of both the Executive Branch and Congress to make patent protection for pharmaceuticals a priority underlines the importance of this industry to the nation's economy. Use of Section 301 of U.S. trade law has been successful in achieving numerous bilateral intellectual property agreements with foreign countries.

Significantly, improvements in intellectual property protection around the world have come not only as a result of U.S. pressure from 301 actions, but because countries understand that intellectual property protection promote their economic interests. The importance of effective patent protection to pharmaceutical innovation indeed is recognized internationally.

The value and significance of Special 301 was attested to on June 15 by Deputy USTR Charlene Barshefsky before the House Foreign Affairs Committee. Ambassador Barshefsky, in describing approaches to promote economic development and growth in the Asia-Pacific region, described two "generic approaches" to attain this end: the GATT Uruguay Round and Special 301. She added that "through the use of Special 301 and the negotiations that are occasioned by the use of that law, we have achieved a literal turnaround in intellectual property protection in Thailand; a turnaround in Korea on intellectual property enforcement; and very substantial gains throughout the ASEAN (Association of Southeast Asian Nations) region . . . (and also in) the Philippines where we have just concluded a very comprehensive set of intellectual property rights agreements."

Ambassador Barshefsky also described the important nexus between economic development and intellectual property by affirming that "without substantial intellectual property rights protection and enforcement, investment flows don't happen, technology transfer doesn't happen, and economic growth is stymied."

We strongly agree with this assessment.

SUCCESSES UNDER SECTION AND SPECIAL 301

There are numerous examples of how the persuasiveness of the U.S. Government, combined with a desire by foreign governments to improve their prospects for economic development, have led to the establishment of pharmaceutical patent protection.

In the Asia-Pacific region, the USTR has been most aggressive in applying the tools of "designation" and "identification" under Special 301. In 1991, the first year in which designation status actually was applied, USTR designated China, India and Thailand as Priority Foreign Countries. In 1992, India and Thailand were re-designated and Taiwan was added to the list of Priority Foreign Countries. In 1993, India and Thailand again were re-designated in this "top" category, and Brazil also was added to this list.

Our industry believes that China, Korea, the Philippines and Taiwan all have improved measures to discourage pharmaceutical piracy as a result of 301-based negotiations.

In Latin America, Mexico's 1991 patent law was the result of that country's economic reform program as well as consultation with the United States. Mexico's new law, in turn, helped pave the way for the historic NAFTA accord. In 1993, Ecuador concluded a bilateral intellectual property agreement with the United States greatly enhancing pharmaceutical patent protection.

In Europe, following difficult negotiations which lasted well over one year, the U.S. entered into an intellectual property agreement with Hungary in August 1993. The Hungarian Patent Law (Hungarian Law VII/94), came into effect in March 1994. It provides for patent protection for pharmaceutical products. Such protection will not hinge on performance (or working) requirements, and provides limitations on the use of compulsory licenses. Also, in these negotiations, the U.S. succeeded in achieving pipeline protection for U.S. products which have filed for a patent no earlier than January 1987.

The terms negotiated between the U.S. and Hungary utilizing Special 301 procedures greatly exceeded those agreed to between Hungary and the European Union. The Europeans managed to obtain only a vague promise that a patent law would be enacted some five years after the agreement, while the U.S.-Hungary Agreement required a patent law to be put into place no later than June 30, 1994.

Notably outside these areas, Egypt also agreed this year to improve patent protection for pharmaceutical products.

Clearly, the web of success that USTR has woven throughout these regions, in cooperation with the U.S. Congress and our industry, has not been a seamless one. There remain several problems in a few "outliers," such as Argentina, Brazil, India and Turkey which so far have refused to adopt patent protection for pharmaceuticals or have failed to live up to earlier commitments to do so.

We also hope that these countries cannot expect to conduct negotiations with the United States to attain improvements in other aspects of their bilateral relationship with the U.S. without having the issue of deficient protection for pharmaceutical products raised as a continuing impediment to such improvements.

We trust that, with the appropriate use of trade "levers" in U.S. trade policy, these countries will adopt effective patent protection for pharmaceutical products as soon as possible. Such levers cannot be used appropriately, however, unless there is better policy coordination between officials within USTR and those in other agencies of the U.S. Government, specifically regarding the employment of bilateral and multilateral trade tools in trying to improve intellectual property protection worldwide.

In the post-Uruguay Round environment, Special 301 can serve as a major point of leverage in these kinds of negotiations and must continue to figure prominently in U.S. policy. Special 301 also serves as an incentive for countries to adopt comprehensive "enforcement" mechanisms, after the appropriate laws have been enacted, to ensure that the laws which have been placed on the "books" do what they say they are going to do.

KEY CHALLENGES

At the end of April, Ambassador Kantor identified 37 trading partners that deny adequate and effective protection of intellectual property or deny fair and equitable market access to U.S. persons that rely upon intellectual property protection. He further indicated that three of these trading partners-Argentina, China and India-pose the most significant problems in this area.

Postponing any immediate designation as Priority Foreign Country, he added that, if a solution to U.S. concerns had not been made by the end of June in these three countries, USTR would designate them as Priority Foreign Countries, and immediately would initiate investigations of their policies, practices and acts under Section 301 of the Trade Act of 1988.

PhRMA member companies would support such designation in two of the countries—India and Argentina—identified by USTR for such designation. Indeed, in the case of India, there is no other country in the world which has played a more insidious and damaging role for such a long period of time in terms of its total disregard for the norms of intellectual property protection, especially for pharmaceutical patents.

This lack of patent protection in India has a very real effect on the number of medicines that are available for Indian citizens to use, and therefore, we believe, on the quality of public health afforded to Indian citizens. For example, of the 434 patented innovative medicines available in the United Kingdom, only 45 are available in India.

While the Indian Government recently implemented a wide-ranging economic liberalization program, it also has excluded the pharmaceutical sector from the benefits of that program. Our industry seeks nothing less than maintenance of India as a Priority Foreign Country and immediate trade action against India for these violations of global trade standards.

In Argentina, we still are awaiting the results of a consideration of draft patent legislation that was re-introduced to the Argentine Senate in May 1993. Although the Government of President Menem has expressed some willingness to speed the process of legislation, there is little indication that an acceptable patent bill will be forthcoming in the near future. If results are not produced by the end of this month, we would encourage the USTR to designate Argentina as a Priority Foreign Country.

In February, the Brazilian Government-made a commitment to improve an existing patent. law by adding amendments which reportedly even would exceed the provisions of the GATT' TRIPs text. During the past five months, these amendments have stalled and there have been no changes to the patents bill. We understand now there are no expectations that there will be any progress in the intellectual property area before the Brazilian October elections. If this is the case, it would represent a broken commitment to the U.S. Government by the Brazilian Government. We then would ask that USTR once again designate Brazil as a Priority Foreign Country.

The Government of Turkey also has promised to enact adequate patent legislation to protect pharmaceutical products. The current draft law contains one major flaw: a four-year delay in implementation. We believe that the U.S. Government should maintain adequate pressure on Turkey to enact an acceptable law, without delayed implementation, by September 1994. If this is not done, USTR should promote Turkey to Priority Foreign Country status.

We also would ask USTR to maintain China on the list of Priority Watch Countries in order to ensure that China fully lives up to its commitments under the U.S.-China Memorandum of Understanding of January 1992.

Although in our Special 301 submission to USTR, we did not suggest that Singapore be elevated to a level above that of Watch Country status, we recently learned that Singapore introduced into its Parliament a new Patents Bill. This bill contains some of the worst compulsory licensing, government use and international exhaustion of rights provisions we have ever seen in any patent legislation.

These provisions in the Patent Bill clearly violate a number of the TRIPs provisions, as well as various aspects of the Paris Convention. In particular, the grant of compulsory licenses based on the reason of non-working in Singapore and the grant of compulsory licenses for food and medicines appear to infringe the geographical and field of technology non-discrimination concept embodied in Article 27 of the TRIPs text.

Last month, PhRMA communicated its concerns about this new law to the Assistant USTR for Asia and the Pacific, as well as to the U.S. Patent and Trademarks Office, and we are currently working with these government agencies to try to improve the patents bill before it actually becomes law.

CONCLUSION

Developments around the world in the past few years have shown that increasing numbers of countries recognize the importance of intellectual property protection to their economic development, and, from the perspective of our industry, to the health of their citizens. Similarly, the U.S. Government and this Subcommittee long have understood the vital role of innovative, high-technology industries such as pharmaceuticals to U.S. economic health.

Patent pirates abroad are resisting this trend in order to protect entrenched domestic interests which thrive on appropriating others' patented technology. Special 301, as well as other 301 provisions, have been successful in stopping or at least reducing such theft in a number of countries.

When it takes effect, the GATT TRIPs accord will provide the legal basis for stopping such theft. In the wake of the Uruguay Round agreement, we must, together, keep up the fight on all fronts and use every available means afforded by U.S. international economic diplomacy to eliminate patent piracy.

PhRMA looks forward to the opportunity to work closely with the Administration and the Congress on Uruguay Round implementing legislation to ensure that the United States retains the ability to enforce intellectual property rights during the delayed implementation period. Given the flaws inherent in the GATT TRIPs text, we would ask that the Congress grant favorable consideration to continued application of Special 301 and other expanded uses of Section 301 legislation.

Mr. Chairman, that concludes my prepared statement. I will be pleased to respond to any questions that you or other Members of the Subcommittee may have.

RESPONSES OF HARVEY E. BALE, JR., TO QUESTION FROM SENATOR GRASSLEY

Question 1. It is my understanding that there may be a transition period for some of the less developed and developing countries in the GATT agreement relative to intellectual property. Can you tell me what effect, if any, these transition periods will have on your individual industry . . . and which countries in particular give you the greatest concern during the transition?

Answer. The GATT Uruguay Round TRIPs agreement includes an overly-long and discriminatory provision allowing many developing countries ten years or more before they must implement pharmaceutical patent protection in accordance with the TRIPs agreement. Furthermore, there is no "pipeline protection" for pharmaceutical patents in TRIPs, in contrast to the NAFTA and numerous other bilateral agreements the United States has reached with other countries. "Pipeline protection" allow for patenting of products that have been patented in one country, e.g., the United States, but not yet marketed in another, e.g., Argentina. Due to the long, 10–12 years between the patenting of a new medicine and its marketing approval, lack of pipeline protection and the delayed implementation period in TRIPS will have serious adverse consequences on the U.S. research-based pharmaceutical industry. In fact, the combination of lack of pipeline protection and ten year implementation delay means that the U.S. innovative pharmaceutical industry will not benefit from TRIPs until well into the 21st century.

As noted in the PhRMA testimony, the most egregious violators of pharmaceutical intellectual property are Argentina, Brazil, India and Turkey. In addition, countries such as Egypt are also significant offenders of intellectual property rights that should not be permitted to delay the implementation of TRIPs.

Question 2. We have all seen countries placed on a priority watch list or a watch list for its failure to enforce intellectual property rights laws and regulations. My question to you is how affective is naming these countries to one of these list in having them come into compliance in your view?

Answer. Naming countries to the Special 301 has proven to be an indispensable and highly effective policy tool of the United States. There are numerous examples of how the persuasiveness of the U.S. Government, combined with a desire by foreign governments to improve their prospects for economic development, have led to the establishment of pharmaceutical patent protection.

Since 1991, the first year in which Special 301 designation was actually made, countries such as *China, Korea, Taiwan, the Philippines* have all improved their protection of pharmaceutical patents. In the Western Hemisphere, *Mexico's* 1991 patent law was the result of that country's economic reform program as well as consultation with the United States. Mexico's new law, in turn, helped pave the way for the historic NAFTA accord. In 1993, *Ecuador* concluded a bilateral intellectual property agreement with the United States greatly enhancing pharmaceutical patent protection.

In Europe, following difficult negotiations which lasted well over one year, the U.S. entered into an intellectual property agreement with *Hungary* in August 1993. The Hungarian Patent Law (Hungarian Law VII/94), came into effect in March 1994.

Question 3. This past April USTR identified 36 trading Partners that deny adequate and effective protection of intellectual property or deny fair and equitable market access to U.S. individuals that rely upon intellectual property protection. Six countries: Japan; Korea; the European Union; Saudi Arabia; Thailand; and Turkey were either placed or retained on the "Priority Watch List." Which of these six pose the greatest threat to your industry and why?

Answer. Turkey, Korea and Thailand remain major problem countries on the Priority Watch List and Saudi Arabia creates concern. Although pharmaceutical patent piracy is not as rife in Saudi Arabia as in other countries on the list, the patent system is relatively new and to our knowledge no pharmaceutical patents have been issued by the Saudi authorities.

In Turkey, the Government has been working on a new patent law for close to two years now and the legislation will likely be referred to the full Parliament this fall. Although we have not yet seen an authoritative translation of the most recent version, we understand that it has several positive provisions. These include a 20-year patent term with no discrimination between imported and domestically produced products, limits on compulsory licensing, protection of proprietary registration data, and a marketing exclusivity provision that provides de facto pipeline protection for pharmaceuticals patented in the United States or other countries but not yet marketed in Turkey. This last provision represents a significant improvement over the Uruguay Round TRIPs text which does not provide pipeline protection for pharmaceuticals. A major flaw in the current draft is that it includes a four-year delay in implementation, which we find unacceptable. If this proposed delayed implementation is eliminated, the draft law will represent considerable progress in the protection of the inventions of U.S. and other research-based companies.

Korea continues to pose significant challenges for the research-based pharmaceutical industry. While the Korean Government adopted effective patent protection and a 10-year pipeline provision for pharmaceutical products in 1987, it continues to restrict access for American inventions in Korea through measures such as denying national treatment for reimbursement for imported pharmaceuticals; imposing restrictive requirements on the registration and promotion of products by non-Korean companies; and inadequate enforcement of the 1987 U.S.-Korean "pipeline" agreement.

Thailand enacted patent law amendments in 1992 which provide 20 years of protection for pharmaceutical products, but which also establish onerous compulsory licensing requirements. Moreover, Thailand's efforts to provide some form of pipeline protection for certain qualifying products which were patented outside of but not marketed within Thailand before 1992 provide no real exclusivity to U.S. products. PhRMA has urged the Thai Government to amend its current law to ensure GATT-compatibility within the next year.

Question 4. I'd like to know how strong each of you feel about the need for Congress to pass a GATT Agreement this year passing a budget waiver to pay for it . . . . if you a beneficiary to GATT, your willingness to shoulder a portion of the burden to pay for a portion of the $40 billion dollar cost?

Answer. PhRMA supports speedy Congressional implementation of the GATT Uruguay Round agreement on the understanding that the United States Government will vigorously continue efforts to improve intellectual property protection in patent-infringing countries. As discussed in PhRMA's June 24 testimony, TRIPs together with the market access agreement eliminating import duties on pharmaceuticals in many major countries, are the two areas of the agreement that have a direct effect on the research-based pharmaceutical industry.

However, while the TRIPs agreement has many positive elements for pharmaceuticals; it also has serious deficiencies. Until many developing countries, such as Argentina, Brazil, India and Turkey, conform their intellectual property regimes to the TRIPs standard, PhRMA and other research-based companies will continue to lose billions of dollars annually to patent pirates. Indeed, in the four countries identified above, PhRMA estimates that U.S. pharmaceutical inventors lose almost $1.5 billion annually. It is regrettable that the Uruguay Round agreement in and of itself does nothing to address the continued patent piracy in these countries for another decade.

Given that the Uruguay Round will increase world trade and benefit the U.S. economy through the elimination and/or lowering of many foreign trade barriers, it is appropriate for the U.S. Government to obtain a budget waiver to deal with the issue of U.S. tariff elimination.

RESPONSES OF HARVEY E. BALE, JR., TO QUESTIONS FROM SENATOR ROTH

Question 1. At the end of April, Ambassador Kantor indicated that he would designate India a Priority Foreign Country under Special 301 unless "solutions to U.S. concerns " were reached with the Indian Government by the end of June. Do you believe that India has done anything to address U.S. concerns in the last two months, and, if not, should India be re-designated as a Priority Foreign Country?

Answer. At the end of June, USTR decided to change India's status from that of Priority Foreign Country to Priority Watch Country. We understand that this decision was made due to the commitment of the Indian Government to improve trademark and copyright protection for American inventions. We have not witnessed any similar progress in the area of patent protection for pharmaceutical products. PhRMA member companies continue to lose around $450 million per annum through piracy of pharmaceutical patents in India, and we continue to view this situation as intolerable. We were, however, encouraged by USTR's recognition in its June statement of India's lack of progress in the patent area.

We also understand that the USTR is planning to engage Indian negotiators in discussions intended to resolve outstanding intellectual property issues, including those affecting our industry, within the next several months. If the Indian Government continues to dig in its heels in ignoring the importance of improved patent protection for pharmaceutical products, we believe that USTR should re-designate India as a Priority Foreign Country and take appropriate trade action against India in lieu of re-launching another Special 301 investigation.

Question 2. If the U.S. Government were to "downgrade" India's status under Special 301 from Priority Foreign Country to Priority Watch status, what kind of effect would this have on U.S. efforts to improve intellectual property protection in other countries, especially Argentina and Brazil?

Answer. PhRMA and its member companies hope that the Indian Government responds to the good faith efforts of the U.S. Government in downgrading India's Special 301 status from Priority Foreign Country to Priority Watch by moving quickly to adopt effective patent protection for pharmaceutical products. If India moves to adopt such protection, USTR's decision to change India's status could have a positive effect on negotiations with Argentina and Brazil.

Question 3. Do you believe that, if the USTR were to re-designate India as a Priority Foreign Country, the U.S. would have more leverage in convincing India to implement the principles of the GATT TRIPs text more quickly than it now appears they are prepared to do, i.e., more quickly than a ten-year delayed implementation? How might this work?

Answer. Since USTR already has changed India's status from Priority Foreign Country to Priority Watch, PhRMA hopes that USTR's commitment to work with the Indian Government to improve protection for pharmaceutical patents during the next few months will result in more rapid adoption of GATT TRIPs principles by the Indian Government. Certainly, we continue to view the allowable ten-year delay in adopting such principles as unacceptable, in India as well in any other GATT signatory country. If India fails to respond to U.S. Government efforts, we believe that the U.S. Government should resort to whatever trade action it deems as necessary to ensure that India moves quickly to adopt GATT principles and to provide pipeline protection for products patented outside of but not yet marketed within India.

Prepared Statement of Jason S. Berman

Good morning Mr. Chairman. Let me begin by thanking you for inviting me this morning, but more importantly for your initiative and interest in holding this hearing in the first place. Over the years, your continued resolve in addressing the piracy of US intellectual property in overseas markets has sent the message to our trading partners that piracy of US works will be subject to trade retaliation, and you have thus assisted the Administration in securing shared goals. Achieving reform of intellectual property practices and obtaining meaningful market access for US intellectual property industries is only possible with the determined, bi-partisan and cooperative effort of Congress, the Administration, and the private sector. Mr. Chairman, you and this Subcommittee have, over the years, more than held up the Congressional end of the bargain.

Let me also take this opportunity to do what gets done far too infrequently—commend USTR for the leadership and commitment that it has demonstrated in what is frequently a thankless job. Day in and day out, Ambassador Kantor and his team have worked tirelessly in an attempt to expand the market opportunities for one of America's greatest exports—the products and services arising from the ingenuity and creativity of her people.

Our creative industries, already important in an industrial age, will become increasingly more critical to our economy in the coming information age. The US must protect its leadership and competitive edge in this critical sector of the world economy. Protecting our competitive edge in this area does not mean preserving the status quo—rather it suggests the need to continue to find creative ways of opening foreign markets and promoting more effective copyright protection. It also suggests reexamining international copyright standards to ensure that they continue to promote investment in the creation and distribution of original works by ensuring that a copyright owner's control over his or her creation is not eliminated by advances in technology.

Section 301, and Special 301 in particular, have been instrumental in raising awareness around the world of the need to adequately and effectively protect intellectual property. Congressional establishment of this tool, used forcefully and imaginatively by USTR since its inception, has led to dramatic growth in the foreign sales of US copyrighted materials. What were once secondary or even unknown markets now have assumed such importance that they figure into the initial marketing and promotion plans for product launches. The amortization of costs over broader markets has, in turn, permitted even greater risk-taking in what have traditionally been high-risk enterprises, resulting in ever increasing levels of creative activity and entrepreneurship.

Developments in intellectual property protection around the world, sparked by thoughtful and determined US bilateral initiatives under Special 301, led to a new binding international discipline within the framework of GATT/TRIPS. GATT/TRIPS, while incomplete, creates a new international benchmark for the protection and enforcement of intellectual property, and thus offers a new launching pad for continued US bilateral initiatives to promote even more effective intellectual property protection.

The task ahead of us is to design a strategy that permits the United States to continue its lonely and inexorable march towards the establishment of favorable market conditions around the world for the development and distribution of creative works. GATT/TRIPS may resolve some questions—such as the rental of sound recordings and computer software and the term of protection. However, it either fails to address, or does so only incompletely, certain other questions, two of which are of central importance—market access for copyright based industries and questions related to the electronic transmission of works through local, regional and global telecommunications systems. We will need to devote an increasing level of attention to these issues that will determine the future competitiveness of US copyright industries, while at the same time addressing the traditional piracy problems that still confront us in many parts of the world.

The ability of the United States to continue to have the capacity to improve market conditions around the world is completely in the hands of you, the Congress. You must ensure that the Administration has the tools to continue the fight for improved global intellectual property protection in a post-Uruguay Round environment. This has a number of components.

First, the USTR must have clear and broad authority to take both trade and non-trade measures in response to the denial of adequate and effective intellectual property protection. Our trading partners must be made aware of our ability *and our intention* to directly address the lack of adequate and effective protection of US copyrighted works. This involves both providing USTR and the President greater discretion to take any action to respond to Special 301 violations, and making clear to the world that "adequate and effective protection" under Special 301 is not limited to those obligations contained in GATT/TRIPS. The modifications of Special 301—in large part merely clarifications of existing authority—should ensure that Special 301 continues to be the forceful catalyst for progress that it has been in the past.

Second, we must strengthen the trade tools that remain unaffected by the Uruguay Round and can serve as important points of leverage in securing improved protection. I am referring, in particular, to GSP, CBI, and other like programs. GSP must be renewed as it provides perhaps the greatest single "trade" remedy available to secure improved protection. Along these' lines Special 301 should be modified to permit USTR to remove country eligibility under GSP pursuant to a determination under Special 301 that a country denies adequate and effective protection of intellectual property. This is an available remedy under GSP, and should be paralleled under Special 301.

Third, Congress needs to work with the Administration in fashioning an unambiguous set of negotiating objectives in the post-Uruguay Round environment. This agenda should clearly set out our intention to use all of the tools available to us, including, where appropriate, recourse to WTO, as well as unilateral measures. We must serve notice to our trading partners that our decision-making under Special 301 about what constitutes adequate and effective intellectual property protection is not affected, in any way, by GATT/TRIPS. What remedies we can fashion to deal with these practices may be affected by the TRIPS Agreement, but not our decision-making about whether a practice unjustifiably, unfairly, or unreasonably denies fair and equitable market access or provision of adequate and effective protection of intellectual property.

Fourth, Congress must move quickly to pass the GATT implementing legislation, demonstrating our commitment to the multilateral trading system and establishing our willingness to maintain a leadership position within the system.

The United States has a great deal to win or lose on this proposition. If we are seen as being dragged unwillingly into a multilateral legal framework, we assume the identity and psychology of the victim, and are sure to fall on tough times ahead. There is far too much at stake and far too many opportunities available to let this happen.

The United States, by passing the GATT implementation bill before summer recess, will be sending an entirely different message to the world. By moving quickly to implement our obligations and at the same time strengthening our ability and resolve to use bilateral and unilateral measures to further US economic objectives, we will succeed in demonstrating by example the sanctity of the international trading system, and our desire to preserve its integrity. The world should expect no less from its greatest trading nation.

In implementing our GATT obligations, and bearing in mind that we will in many instances be setting an example for others to follow, it is critical that we broadly interpret our obligations in certain key areas. The United States has traditionally done so in the copyright arena, and it must maintain this valuable tradition In particular, the US must broadly construe Article 18 of the Berne Convention by restoring protection to foreign works now in the public domain as was done in NAFTA, and must establish a federal anti-bootleg statute. Too frequently in the past, our trading partners have, for the most part disingenuously, cited the narrower interpretation of the Berne Implementation Act to justify not protecting preexisting US works, even though the market implications of this de jure parallelism are completely disparate; and US performers and the record companies for whom they record have too frequently been denied protection because our trading partners have failed to account for the protection available at the state level and have merely identified a lack of federal protection in relation to live performances. It is time to stop these practices by amending our own laws. We have a great deal to gain as the world's largest exporter of recorded music and other copyrighted materials.

Finally, Mr. Chairman, Congress must continue oversight on the Administration's use of the trade tools that you have fashioned for their use. I say this not as a way of putting pressure on the Administration, for as I said earlier, I think that USTR has made creative, aggressive and positive use of available tools. Rather; by maintaining continuing and interested oversight in the process, you strengthen USTR's hand in negotiations by demonstrating the resolve of the entire US Government in addressing intellectual property and market access.

By passing the GATT implementing legislation including modifications of some US copyright practices, as well as amendments to trade legislation to ensure that the Administration continues to have tools with which to promote US economic interests bilaterally, and by continuing to demonstrate your interest in ensuring that USTR is able to successfully wage war against copyright piracy and closed markets, you will be defining a strategy that will take us profitably and competitively into the next century.

In closing, I just want to note one important event that will arise next week. As you are well aware, USTR must decide by June 30 if China, Argentina and India are denying adequate and effective protection within the meaning of Special 301. In announcing postponement of his decision in April, Ambassador Kantor noted that China and the others would be designated if "solutions" to the problems that had been identified were not resolved. From my perspective, a "solution" means that China's 26 plus CD plants are no longer producing pirate CDs, either for local consumption or export, and that the Chinese have demonstrated their willingness and ability to fight piracy. In the absence of meeting these conditions, it is critical that China be identified on June 30, and I urge you to communicate to the Administration your support of this position.

Thank you for this opportunity to discuss these important issues, and I look forward to answering any questions that you may have.

RESPONSES FROM JASON S. BERMAN TO QUESTIONS FROM SENATOR GRASSLEY

July 28, 1994.

Hon. CHARLES E. GRASSLEY,
U.S. Senate,
135 Senate Hart Office Building,
Washington, DC

Dear Senator Grassley: I am pleased to provide the following responses to your questions regarding my testimony on June 24 at the hearing on Special 301.

Question 1. It is my understanding that there may be a transition period for some of the less developed and developing countries in the GATT agreement relative to intellectual property. Can you tell me what effect, if any, these transition periods will have on your individual industry . . . and which countries in particular give you the greatest concern during the transition?

Answer. The long transition periods available to some countries under the GATT Agreement are potentially exceedingly problematic for the US record industry and other copyright-based industries. Unlike other areas of intellectual property, meeting the substantive obligations of TRIPS in respect of *copyright* does not require the establishment of regulatory or administrative mechanisms. There is thus no justification for permitting any country more than one year to legislate and enforce copyright protection. The US copyright industries lose *15–17* billion dollars a year to piracy. Each year of transition carries with it a huge loss to US businesses and the US economy as a whole.

It is thus critical that Section 301 permit the Administration to address this deficiency in the GATT Agreement by providing that TRIPS compliance does not equate to "adequate and effective" protection under Special 301. It is also critical to identify shortening the transition period in individual negotiations with foreign countries as a primary negotiating objective of the Administration.

In terms of which countries give us the greatest concern, I would say that we are very concerned that China will seek to use the transition period to avoid existing bilateral obligations, and that it is critical that the United States secure agreement from China with respect to transition on intellectual property during the working party discussions on China's WTO accession.

Question 2. We have all seen countries placed on a priority watch list or a watch list for its failure to enforce intellectual property rights laws and regulations. My question to you is how affective is naming these countries to one of these list in having them come into compliance in your view?

Answer. The creative use by USTR of the statutory tools created by Congress in the 1988 Trade Act, an in particular Special 301, has been very effective in achieving progress with respect to the protection of intellectual property. In many instances the naming of countries to lists as opposed to designating them as "priority foreign countries" has been sufficient to get countries to address our concerns, and in other instances it has not been so successful. Overall, the ability of USTR to identify its priorities in this manner has been instrumental in promoting reform by giving countries notice of our intention and permitting the escalation or de-escalation of trade pressure.

Question 3. This past April USTR identified 36 trading Partners that deny adequate and effective protection of intellectual property or deny fair and equitable market access to U.S. individuals that rely upon intellectual property protection. Six countries: Japan; Korea; the European Union; Saudi Arabia; Thailand; and Turkey were either placed or retained on the "Priority Watch List." Which of these six pose the greatest threat to your industry and why?

Answer. Each of these countries, with the possible exception of Korea, pose some threat to the US record industry. Japanese rental practices, permissible even under the GATT Agreement which precludes any other country from engaging in unauthorized rental, continue to prejudice US record companies and performers, and Japanese copyright law continues to discriminate against US record companies and performers with respect to broadcasting and public performance rights.

The European Union, and the members thereof, have been our primary adversary in trying to introduce a broad rule of national treatment in respect of all rights in the copyright arena—including private copying levies and broadcasting and public performance rights. Members of the EU have discriminated against US interests by denying US access to existing rights and revenues. The EU's "cultural policy" also operates to limit our access to the European market.

Saudi Arabia continues to be a major market for pirate tapes, and Saudi authorities have done little to enforce the provisions of a copyright law that was passed within the last few years. Saudi Arabia has only recently adhered to the Universal Copyright Convention, and we eagerly await a new enforcement regime.

Thailand has recently done a much better job of enforcing its copyright laws and piracy is on the wane. We have great concerns, however, about a rising tide of CD piracy, and we are carefully monitoring the government's response to this new challenge.

Turkey's piracy rate has mushroomed in recent years, and the government has demonstrated little resolve in addressing it. A new copyright law has been debated for years, and there appears to be no immediate change on the horizon.

Question 4. I'd like to know how strong each of you feel about the need for Congress to pass a GATT Agreement this year passing a budget waiver to pay for it . . . . if you a beneficiary to GATT, your willingness to shoulder a portion of the burden to pay for a portion of the $40 billion dollar cost?

Answer. It is absolutely critical that Congress pass the GATT Agreement this year, both to secure the economic gains that will flow to the United States under the Agreement, and to demonstrate the willingness of the United States to maintain its leadership position in its international commercial relations. Given the ultimate value to the United States of GATT implementation, we would support to budget waiver to pay the "costs" associated with the legislation. These "costs" will be more than offset by the economic gains of the Agreement. Bearing in mind that there are no real "costs" associated with GATT implementation, we are in no position to respond to your question about bearing some of these putative costs to pay for the Agreement.

Please contact me if I can clarify anything further.

Sincerely,

JASON S. BERMAN.

PREPARED STATEMENT OF SENATOR CHARLES E. GRASSLEY

Thank you Mr. Chairman:

I believe this is the second hearing we have had on special 301 this year and I would like to once again commend your efforts in this very vital trade issue.

The United States products and ideas in many respects represent the highest level of technology creativity in the world. When the intellectual property of Americans is not protected, our country loses jobs, profits, a higher standard of living.

For these reasons alone, it is expressly important for the United States to be able to identify those countries that deny adequate and effective protection of intellectual property rights or deny fair or equitable market access to U.S. exporters that rely on intellectual property protection.

As you know, Mr. Chairman, intellectual property products are broadly divided into three types: copyrights; patents; and trademarks. As a member of this committee and the Judiciary Committee I will be taking a close look at the implementing language of the GATT agreement to ensure adequate protection is provided.

When Congress enacted special 301 as part of the 1988 TRADE ACT, U. S. owners of intellectual property faced extensive piracy in other countries. While the statute has worked particularly well in helping U.S. negotiators persuade countries to adopt changes in their laws to bring them up to international standards, this is but a first step. Now we must vigorously pursue the goal and commitment to improve protection, strengthen enforcement, and remove barriers to market access. We must also include deadlines and benchmarks for evaluating a country's performance, in the event that problems remain unresolved, if we are to have an effective action plan.

I look forward to the testimony of today's witnesses and the comments of my colleagues.

Thank you Mr. Chairman.

PREPARED STATEMENT BY SENATOR ORRIN G. HATCH

Mr. Chairman, I appreciate the opportunity to address the subcommittee today on a topic that is of great importance to me. I believe that Special 301 is critical to our nation's industries that rely on adequate protection of intellectual property.

As you know, the United States has led the world in the development of intellectual property, and I am pleased with the general progress that has been made over the years in bringing other countries, especially those less developed economies, to impose and enforce a reasonable standard of protection.

However, as I know the witness panel will assure us today, there are still egregious violations around the world that need to be addressed. Therefore, as we continue to establish and improve international standards for Trade Related Intellectual Property Measures (TRIPS) in GATT, we must, in the meantime maintain credible and effective mechanisms to protect an important portion of our nation's economy until those standards are properly adhered to by all nations.

I look forward to hearing the comments of today's witnesses.

PREPARED STATEMENT OF ROBERT W. HOLLEYMAN II

Mr. Chairman: It is a privilege to have the opportunity to appear again before this subcommittee. The Business Software Alliance (BSA) represents the leading publishers of software for personal computers, including Aldus, Apple Computer, Autodesk, Intergraph, Lotus, Microsoft, Novell and WordPerfect. Collectively, these companies account for nearly three-quarters of the sales of packaged software published by U.S. companies. U.S. software companies, in turn, account for approximately 74 percent of worldwide software sales. BSA members receive, on average, in excess of 50 percent of their annual revenues from foreign sales. An effective U.S. trade policy is a critical element in the success of software companies abroad, and there has been no more important trade instrument in recent years than the Special 301 provisions of the 1988 Trade Act.

This hearing raises two fundamental questions. First, how well has Special 301 been implemented in the most recent series of designations, looking at China in particular? Second, what is the future of Special 301 in light of the new World Trade Organization and the intellectual property component of the Uruguay Round? Finally, I would like to raise a third point, with respect to Japan, showing the progress that can be achieved through well implemented trade policy, including effective use of Special 301.

The 1994 Designations

This year, the BSA, through our membership in the International Intellectual Property Alliance, recommended that 32 countries be identified in one of the three Special 301 categories: Priority Foreign Country, Priority Watch List, or Watch List. Losses to U.S. software publishers in these countries exceeded $2.8 billion in 1993. Overall software piracy losses are even higher in each of the recommended countries, when the losses to the local distribution channel and the foreign publishers' share are added to the picture. A list of the recommended countries is attached, with a chart showing U.S. software losses in each, including five countries identified by IIPA for "special comment" because of problems, albeit ones not rising to the level of the three lists.

On April 30, U.S. Trade Representative Mickey Kantor announced that six U.S. trading partners were being placed on the Priority Watch List and nineteen on the Watch List. Nine countries were identified for continuing or prospective. problems, although not rising to the level of one of the three traditional categories. Finally, USTR chose to defer until June 30 decisions on three trading partners—Argentina, China and India—being considered for Priority Foreign Country status.

All of the countries recommended in the IIPA/BSA submission were identified by Ambassador Kantor in some fashion with several exceptions: South Africa and Uruguay, for which Watch List status had been sought, plus Mexico and Malaysia, the subject of IIPA "special comments."

CHINA

Of the three countries being considered for Priority Foreign Country designation on June 30, the most critical to software is China. The U.S. software industry had direct losses of $322 million in China in 1993. Ninety-four percent of all the packaged software in use in China is estimated to be pirated, according to BSA research examining the total hardware units sold in comparison with the total software packages sold, and estimated applications in use within that country last year.

China poses a particularly difficult problem for software. It is a country we applauded when, in 1992, China reached a bilateral agreement with the U.S. that called for copyright protection for foreign and domestic software, and adherence to the Berne Convention. As part of the Memorandum of Understanding (MOU) that was executed, the Chinese Government committed to "provide effective procedures and remedies to prevent or stop, internally and at their borders, infringement of intellectual property rights and to deter further infringements."

Sadly, the commitment to enforcement laid out in the MOU has not been fulfilled. Software piracy remains rampant in China, despite underlying legal protection. In March of this year, BSA filed its first cases against a number of software dealers in one of the PRC's new Intellectual Property tribunals. However, BSA effort bring enforcement actions against software piracy in the retail marketplace have foundered for months in the face of a legal system that makes it seemingly impossible to initiate and carry .out raids to confiscate pirated goods in either a timely or cost-effective fashion. I would like to emphasize that we have spent months simply trying to have raids executed. We have identified the targets, we have verified information that pirated software is being sold, and we have filed complaints with the courts. Yet, the requested raids have not yet been carried out, and our expenses mount—graduated filing fees, attorneys fees, on and on. One hates to think of the further delays and difficulties that may be encountered as we seek to have the cases adjudicated, assuming that the raids are ultimately carried out.

For these and other reasons, coupled with the lack of criminal penalties for infringement, the BSA joined with our allied organizations in the IIPA in recommending that China again be designated as a Priority Foreign Country in 1994. As our cases have dragged on, so too have we come to recognize that trade pressure from the U.S. may be the only real means we have to see that the Chinese carry out their commitments to enforcement. Just as it took a Priority Foreign Country designation and investigation to cause China to protect foreign works, and accede to Berne, so too have we come to recognize it may take yet another designation to get the Chinese to carry out commitments to enforcement.

BSA knows that a U.S. Government negotiating team has been in China last week and this one, seeking assurances that could avoid another designation. Regrettably, software's experience shows that much remains to be done, and it seems unlikely from this vantage point that the Chinese Government will make the extensive changes and commitments that we believe should be required to avoid designation next week, nor do we believe that promises given now will be adequate in light of the countless delays we have experienced in simply trying to have initial raids executed.

As is known, the Clinton Administration deferred designating China as a Priority Foreign Country on April 30 because of the then-pending decision on renewal of Most Favored Nation status for the P.R.C. BSA did not agree with that deferral. We felt that the statutorily-mandated timetable for making decisions under the 1988 Act should have been met, and we communicated our position to USTR before the decision was made.

Nonetheless, we recognize that MFN overshadowed other considerations, even one as critically important as ending piracy and protecting U.S. intellectual property in China. So, with considerable reluctance we acknowledged the decision made within the highest levels of the U.S. Government, trusting that it would never again be used as a precedent for future designations. We recognized, too, that some of the leverage gained from Special 301 may have been compromised by delay. The time to determine whether that can be salvaged is now at hand—next week to be precise.

As time—and our cases—have worn on, we have become increasingly convinced that Priority Foreign Country status will almost certainly be required for China to make progress in protecting software. We call on Ambassador Kantor to make that decision by the announced date of June 30. For the U.S., it would be a terrible loss if those very software companies that have achieved success in other markets abroad, failed to gain real access to the world's most populous market. China offers a market where personal computers are just now gaining a foothold and where software developed by U.S. companies could achieve widespread acceptance if that software can be marketed and piracy reduced. To that end, BSA awaits the Administration's forthcoming decision.

WTO

Questions have been raised about the future of Special 301 in light of the new World Trade Organization and conclusion of the Uruguay Round. Let me say at the outset that the BSA views the successful inclusion of trade-related intellectual property (TRIPs) requirements in the final agreement as a major victory for the software industry and the U.S. economy. Software was the fastest growing major industry over the period 1982–1992, growing by 269 percent in real terms, while the remainder of the economy grew by about 30 percent. The total computer software industry now accounts for $36.7 billion in value added to the U.S. economy, and is larger than all but five of this nation's manufacturing industries.

The GATT agreement represents the best way for the U.S. to preserve—and enhance—the gains that have been made for software through bilateral negotiations. The TRIPs text encompasses many of the provisions that the U.S. has sought over the last decade or more, including protection for software under copyright as a literary work, for a term of 50 years, coupled with enforcement obligations. Adoption of the TRIPs requirements would do much to enhance the already competitive posture of the U.S. software industry on a worldwide basis; and the BSA strongly supports Congressional approval of the accord.

What is to become of Special 301 in a WTO environment? Much debate has surrounded this question. For its part, BSA shares the view of allied organizations within the IIPA that while strong, the TRIPs standards of protection are not the same, indeed are lower, than the "adequate and effective protection" standards required by Section 301, Special 301 and other U.S. trade programs.

With this in mind, we have three current recommendations. First, Special 301 should be used now to accelerate the compliance of developing countries with TRIPs obligations, despite the existence of a four-year and ten-year transition period for Less Developed Countries (LDCs) and Least Developed Countries (LLDCs), respectively.

Second, Special 301 should be used to address issues which were not resolved in the Uruguay Round. U.S. bilateral accords should seek full national treatment for all U.S. works, parallel import protection, and elimination of market barriers that were not addressed in the Round and which will not be addressed through the WTO.

Finally, while we are concerned that the scope of Special 301 may be narrower with the WTO in place, the U.S. has additional mechanisms that should be employed to supplement Special 301 and to secure full protection for intellectual property (IP). Two programs—the Generalized System of Preferences (GSP) and the Caribbean Basin Initiative (CBI), immediately come to mind. Other devices such as bank loans and financial programs may also be used to achieve trade objectives. BSA urges that these and other programs be expanded to encompass IP trade objectives, in conjunction with the WTO and a narrower Special 301. Even though this will pose challenges, taken as a whole, BSA believes that the ability to protect software on an international basis will be greatly enhanced with implementation of the

TRIPs requirements. We fully support efforts by the Clinton Administration and the Congress to approve GATT implementing legislation at the earliest possible date.

JAPAN

Finally, let me conclude with a word of thanks and a very recent example showing where Special 301 and U.S. trade policy has been used effectively for the benefit of software.

Last November, I testified before this committee regarding a serious threat that had arisen for U.S. software companies in Japan. The threat was posed by the establishment of a study commission within the Japanese Ministry of Education (Cultural Affairs Agency) to consider possible changes in the Japanese copyright law affecting software.

The Japanese law was amended in 1985 to secure copyright protection for software, following intensive bilateral negotiations with the U.S. With a law in place, U.S. software companies doing business in Japan have seen rapid growth in their market share in that country, with most recent estimates suggesting a 60 percent and growing market share for U.S. packaged products.

In the face of that growing market share, efforts arose within Japan to consider amendments to the Japanese law to weaken protection for software. Testimony before the study commission advocated amending the law to allow, without the consent of the copyright owner, commercial decompilation of computer programs—meaning, to allow programs to be taken from their object code (the machine readable form) back into source code (the human readable form), an act which requires intermediate copying. This became a very controversial exercise, with the vast majority of U.S. software and hardware interests speaking in opposition to changes in the current law. On the other hand, Keidanren, the Japanese Federation of Industries, submitted comments to the study commission advocating amendments to the Japanese copyright law to authorize decompilation "for any purpose" with the stated reason to "avoid redundant investments in technology." To U.S. software companies, whose products have gained widespread consumer acceptance in Japan, this posed a very tangible and serious threat to our ability to do business in that country, and indeed around the world were a software clone industry to arise and expand through changes in law in other countries.

I am pleased to report that members of the Senate, including the Chairman of this subcommittee, the House, and representatives of the Administration, recognized the severity of the threat in Japan and took action. The software decompilation issue was identified as a matter of "gravest concern," in the words of Ambassador Charlene Barshefsky. Ambassador Kantor and Secretary Ron Brown raised this matter in letters to their Japanese counterparts. Ambassador Mondale championed the U.S. Government's position on the ground in Tokyo. Members of Congress expressed their strong support for this position. Most recently, Japan was elevated to the Priority Watch List under Special 301, in large part because of the decompilation study and the 80 percent rate of software piracy.

All of this bore fruit last month when the Ministry of Education released its report. That report made clear that a "definitive conclusion" on decompilation could not be reached by the study commission and recommended that it would be "more appropriate to wait for the development of case law and academic theory" and "reexamine the situation in view of future domestic and overseas developments," prior to recommending statutory revisions.

The report's conclusion does not mean that the threat has passed forever, but it signals a very significant interim victory. Having been in Tokyo in both October and December of last year, and through reports from many in our industry who have been there in the intervening months, I can say that this victory would not have been achieved without the direct intervention and involvement of the U.S. Government. The threat has not passed forever, but it has been removed for the immediate future. This signals good things for the U.S. software industry and serves as an example of what can be achieved through a well-managed confluence of overall trade policy, Hill involvement, support from all quarters within the Administration, and Special 301.

Thank you for this opportunity to testify.

ATTACHMENT-A (ROBERT W. HOLLEYMAN, TESTIMONY)

(Revised 5/9/94)

USTR "SPECIAL 301" DECISIONS FOR 1994 AND IIPA ESTIMATED TRADE LOSSES DUE TO PIRACY (1993)
(in millions)

	Motion Pictures	Records & Music	Computer Programs	Books	Total
****See Note Below****					
People's Republic of China	50	345	322	110	827
India	40	45	81	25	191
Argentina	34	10	55	5	104
Priority Watch List					
Japan	95	NA	807	3	905
Korea	20	20	371	12	423
Saudi Arabia	79	43	57	7	186
Turkey (GSP)	35	12	103	14	164
Thailand	20	12	98	25	155
European Union	NA	NA	NA	NA	NA
Watch List					
Italy	357	38	186	NA	581
Spain	53	NA	191	10	254
Poland (GSP)	45	24	159	15	243
Indonesia	45	12	95	40	192
Taiwan	26	6	106	12	150
United Arab Emirates★	7	108	27	2	144
Australia	33	12	77	1.5	123.5
Venezuela	40	12	51	20	123
Philippines	23	15	NA	70	108
Greece★	55	15	33	4	107
Egypt (GSP)★	11	4	52	17	84

★: Subject to Out-of-Cycle Review by USTR.
GSP: GSP review of IPR practices pending.

April 30, 1994

Note: USTR has delayed a final decision on the identification of the PRC, India and Argentina as "Priority Foreign Countries" until June 30, 1994.

USTR "SPECIAL 301" DECISIONS FOR 1994 AND IIPA ESTIMATED TRADE LOSSES DUE TO PIRACY (1993) (in millions)

(Revised 5/9/94)

	Motion Pictures	Records & Music	Computer Programs	Books	Total
Watch List - continued					
Pakistan	20	30	3	25	78
Cyprus (GSP)	29	4	3	15	51
Peru	0.2	13	12	10	35.2
El Salvador★(GSP)	1.7	6	NA	1	8.7
Guatemala (GSP)	0.7	1	NA	1	2.7
Chile	NA	NA	NA	NA	NA
Colombia	NA	NA	NA	NA	NA
Subtotal	1119.6	787	2889	444.5	5240.1
Special Mention					
Germany	53	70	909	NA	1032
Russian Federation	40	300	49	55	444
Brazil	39	36	190	30	295
Israel	12	9	18	3	42
Singapore	1	3	21	2	27
Paraguay	0.2	NA	8	2	10.2
Panama	1.6	0.5	2	2	6.1
Honduras (GSP)	0.7	0.5	NA	1	2.2
Canada	NA	NA	NA	NA	NA
Subtotal	147.5	419	1197	95	1858.5
Total	1267.1	1206	4086	539.5	7098.6

★: Subject to Out-of-Cycle Review by USTR.

GSP: GSP review of IPR practices pending.

April 30, 1994

Note: Chile, Colombia and Canada were not included in IIPA recommendations to USTR in February 1994 and estimated trade losses are not available at this time.

Responses of Robert W. Holleyman II to Questions From Senator Hatch

Question 1. As you know, Argentina is currently being considered by USTR to be designated a priority country next week. Could you share with the subcommittee specific examples of what your association members are dealing with in trying to do business in Argentina?

Answer. Other than the high piracy rate, the software industry's major challenge in Argentina comes from a sudden change last year when Argentine Customs began trying to assess its high (25%) duty over the full value of the software package (value of the physical diskettes plus the intellectual content). Before this sudden change, Argentine Customs had assessed the duty only over the value of the physical media. as is done in virtually all major countries (please see Table 2, of the attached letter from BSA to USTR). In addition, the BSA has encountered procedural problems in pursuing anti-piracy litigation in Argentina, including the inability to obtain ex parte searches in civil litigation and the difficulty of determining damages for infringement. Both civil and criminal cases suffer from an overburdened and extremely slow court system.

Question 2. How does Argentina compare with other nations, where your association members are facing IPR violations, in terms of the dollar amounts of the various violations?

Answer. The Business Software Alliance estimates 74 percent of the software programs in use in Argentina are pirated, leading to $55 million in direct losses to U.S. publishers in 1993 (please see the attached chart for a comparison with other countries). Total piracy losses experienced by U.S., Argentine and foreign publishers, and the Argentine distributors of software approached $112 million last year.

Question 3. Do you believe that the process currently underway in the Argentine legislative body will be effective in curbing the abuses you cite (assuming adequate enforcement)?

Answer. BSA is not aware of any Argentine legislative initiatives in the area of copyright that would affect software piracy. BSA is encouraged by the recent Decree (165/94, February 3, 1994) signed by President Menem which confirms the copyrightability of computer programs and databases as literary works. This should strengthen our ability to bring copyright infringement actions. There is currently no legislation pending that would provide relief for the customs valuation problem.

GATT TRIPs Agreement

Question 1. I would be interested in knowing what specific areas, if any, you believe the GATT implementing language could be helpful in improving the way in which we interpret the TRIPs provision in the Uruguay Round? Is the Uruguay Round TRIPs text satisfactory?

Answer. Regarding the GATT agreement, BSA is generally pleased with the final agreement signed last December. As was stated in our testimony, the GATT TRIPs text encompasses many of the provisions that the U.S. has sought over the last decade or more, including protection for software under copyright as a literary work, for a term of 50 years, coupled with enforcement obligations. Implementation of the TRIPs requirements would be a major boost for the software industry. BSA, along with the other copyright industries, has advocated GATT implementing language that explicitly states, among other positions: that countries do not meet the "adequate and effective protection" test of Section 301 and GSP merely by adherence to TRIPs, and that retaliation against unfair trade practices is not limited to trade only, but can include non-trade measures.

Question 2. What specific areas of the GATT TRIPs text would you recommend addressing in future GATT rounds?

Answer. In future negotiations, BSA would like the U.S. to advance parallel import protection, complete national treatment provisions and the strongest possible standards to ensure adequate and effective enforcement.

Business Software Alliance

2001 L Street N.W.
Suite 400
Washington, D.C. 20036
TEL 202.872.5500
FAX 202.872.5501

VIA FACSIMILE 16 June 1994
ORIGINAL BY COURIER

Ms. Carmen Suro-Bredie
Assistant U.S.T.R. for Latin America, the Caribbean and Africa
Thomas Robertson, Esquire
Assistant General Counsel
Office of the United States Trade Representative
Executive Office of the President
600 Seventeenth Street, NW
Washington, DC 20506

Re: **Serious Argentine Customs Barrier to Sales of U.S.-Origin Software**

Dear Ms. Suro-Bredie and Mr. Robertson:

1. **The Problem.** In response to your request, I can now provide a more comprehensive explanation of the problem faced by U.S. industry since Argentine Customs began trying to assess its high (25%) duty on computer software over the full value of a computer software package (value of the physical diskettes plus the intellectual content) about a year ago. For many years before this sudden change, Argentine Customs had assessed the duty only over the value of the physical media, as is done in virtually all major countries (see Table 2, attached hereto).

It bears mention that Argentine Customs effected this change without appropriate notice to Argentine or foreign businesses, creating a very unstable business climate. Moreover, there is no clear guidance about how far back Customs intends to apply this sudden change. Despite talks between Argentine software distributors, Argentine Customs and other agencies of the Argentine Government, no progress has been reported, and Argentine Customs continues to try to collect the duty over the full value of computer software imports.

In fact, the duty stated in Argentine tariff schedules is 15%, but Argentine Customs adds an additional duty of 10% called *Tasa de Estadística* (statistical rate), resulting in a 25% duty that is among the highest in Latin America (and indeed, the world). The high duty rate is particularly troublesome when applied over the full transaction value of a software package.

This problem, which affects most U.S. software companies that do business in Argentina in a fundamental way (I am told that Microsoft Corp., Lotus Development Corp., IBM, Oracle, Novell, Inc. and WordPerfect Corp., among others, are seriously affected), creates a serious barrier to these important U.S. exports by substantially raising the cost of software to users in Argentina. Moreover, Argentine Customs has been trying to collect the duty over past shipments (generally going back up to one year). This imposes a serious financial burden on Argentine distributors for U.S. companies, which could be seen as a domestic Argentine problem. However, this practice would substantially increase the cost of U.S.-origin software to Argentine users, thus creating a barrier to software sales.

At present, Argentine distributors for U.S. companies are able to redeem software packages from Customs by paying the duty only over the value of the physical media because the industry association filed an *impugnación* or opposition to the new procedure, which has not yet been resolved. Regarding current imports, the Argentine Government proposed reducing the duty to "0%" at the end of last year. However, a resolution to this effect initiated at the Ministry of Economics in January was never signed. The computer software industry does not know what the Argentine Government plans to do.

2. **The Impact.** To evaluate the impact of the new Argentine practice, please see Table 1, attached hereto. The Table assumes that an Argentine distributor has imported a U.S. software package with a CIF value of $100. The value of the media might average about 10% of the value of the package, or $10. Previously, Argentina followed majority practice in collecting its 25% duty over the $10 value of the physical media. The importing distributor thus paid a duty of $2.50. No Customs duty was assessed over the value of the intellectual content or intellectual property of the software package, which has a $90 value in this example.

However, the Argentine distributor does not pay the U.S. software manufacturer $100; the distributor withholds Argentine income tax of 10.75% over the $90 value of the intellectual property, an amount that equals $9.68 in this example. The importing Argentine distributor then pays the U.S. software manufacturer $90.32, and gives the manufacturer a foreign tax certificate in the amount of $9.68 so that the U.S. manufacturer can claim a foreign tax credit (if available to the manufacturer) on its U.S. income tax.

Assuming that the price to the end user will be about 43% greater than the wholesale price, an industry-reasonable assumption for Argentina, the distributor has paid $100 ($90.32 to the software manufacturer and $9.68 to the tax authorities) plus $2.50 in

Customs duty, for a total of $102.50. Thus, a retail price of approximately $146 can be anticipated.

However, if the 25% duty is assessed over the entire value of the package, then the Argentine distributor pays $25 in Customs duties, or a total of $125, which would result in a much higher retail price (perhaps $179), and as one might expect at a higher price, fewer sales. Moreover, if the duty is applied retroactively to the value of the entire software package, then the Argentine distributor is asked to pay an additional $22.50 in Customs duties in the above example, but the distributor has already paid (on behalf of the manufacturer) $9.68 in withholding tax, for total Argentine assessments of $34.68 over a product with a wholesale cost of only $100. This demonstrates the significant adverse impact of the new Argentine Customs practice.

3. **International Guidance.** Under the General Agreement on Tariffs and Trade (GATT), the new Argentine Customs practice is not illegal, but is one of two possible methods for valuation, because "transaction value" is the standard method of customs valuation for most goods. The GATT Committee on Customs Valuation[1] specifically addressed the issue of the customs valuation of software during its Tenth Meeting, September 24, 1984.[2] While the Committee adopted a Decision (Decision 4.1) that allows software to be valued in either of two methods pursuant to Article VII of GATT,[3] the Committee endorsed "split invoicing"–which requires import duties to be paid only on the media–as opposed to upon the full transactional valuation of the software (media and content).[4] The Committee's rationale for allowing the media invoicing of software is persuasive: (1) because software programming could be transmitted via cables and telephone lines (where it would not be subject to any import duty) it is fair to value imported software only as to the media on which it is transmitted (e.g., the value of the diskettes or tape), and (2) the carrier medium is usually a temporary means of storing instructions or data; in order to use the data, the buyer has to transfer or reproduce the data or instructions into the memory or data-base of his own system.

The European Union's (EU, formerly EC) customs value rules have explicitly adopted a software valuation that includes only the cost of the media (and then the tariff is 0%).[5]

---

[1] The Committee is charged to interpret provisions of GATT, but is not empowered to change the terms of the Treaty. S. Sherman & H. Glashoff, Customs Valuation, Commentary on the GATT Customs Valuation Code 56 (1988).

[2] *Id.* at 275 (copy of attached).

[3] Agreement on Implementation of Article VII of the General Agreement on Tariffs and Trade, Part I, Rules on Customs Valuations. General Agreement on Tariffs and Trade, Basic Instruments and Selected Documents, 26th Supp., March 1980.

[4] The Committee is not entitled to change the Customs Valuation Code as such; its Decisions are only recommendations for the interpretation of the Code. But interpretations should be applied retroactively, and the new interpretation should be applied "in all cases in which the duty assessment procedure is still open." S. Sherman & H. Glashoff, supra note 1, Transaction Value of the Imported Goods, 143.

[5] European Community Council Regulation 1055/85; April 23, 1985. *See also* Izzet M. Sinan, *European Community Customs Duties: A Significant Trading Consideration for U.S. Companies*, 18 Wm. Mitchell L.Rev. 401 (1992).

The EU's Valuation Methods were created in response to the Tokyo Round of GATT and mirror many of the GATT provisions.[6] The U.S. Commerce Department's Tariffs and Other Taxes on Computer Hardware and Software (May 1994) lists the customs valuation for software for EU countries as media only with a 0% duty rate. For software designated as "multimedia" there is a 5.1% duty rate.[7]

The United States imposes a duty only over the physical value of the media. Canada allows importers to separately value media and content, and assesses duties only over the value of the media. Software on diskettes enters Canada duty free.[8] Other software entering Canada (e.g., software imbedded in hardware) is virtually duty free pursuant to Canada's Computer Carrier Media Remission Order,[9] which allows separate calculations for the carrier medium, instructions, information or data contained on the medium, and the value of reproducing the instructions on the medium.[10]

Table 2 summarizes the data obtained regarding the customs valuation of software for Canada, Brazil, Chile, Mexico, France, United Kingdom, Germany, Japan, Spain, and the United States. Every country but Chile on the list limits the assessment of duties on software to the value of the carrier media only. In addition, such countries as Taiwan, Hong Kong, Australia and even Russia limit duty assessment to the value of the media. If Argentina adopts a content valuation scheme it will clearly be out of step with its North American and European trading partners, and will instead align itself with a distinct minority of underdeveloped countries found primarily in Latin America (Peru, Bolivia, Ecuador), Africa and India. I also attach a U.S. Department of Commerce document called "Tariffs and Other Taxes on Computer Hardware and Software" to the mailed copy of this letter.

The strong international trend, which Argentina has recently chosen to resist, is definitely to value only the transport media of the software for Customs purposes, treating the intellectual content as data that could enter the country through other duty-free means and, therefore, not imposing a value for customs purposes on such content.

4. **Request.** On behalf of the Business Software Alliance, we certainly would appreciate your assistance in opposing this substantial (if not illegal) market barrier to U.S.-origin software, as it clearly does not comport with Argentina's putative interest in free trade and free markets. Argentina's recent Customs policy shift runs counter to the

---

[6] Sinan, *supra* note 4, at "VI. Valuation of Goods." Countries currently members of the EU are France, Germany, Italy, Belgium, the Netherlands, Luxembourg, United Kingdom, Denmark, Ireland, Greece, Spain, and Portugal.

[7] Telephone Conversation with Mary Smolenski, U.S. Commerce Department, June 2, 1994 ((202)482-0551)(relating that software containing audiovisual elements are reportedly subject to the higher tax rate and that the exact status of this tax is not certain).

[8] C. Ian Kyer, *Marketing Computers and Software in Canada*, 259 Practicing Law Institute/Patents 449, PAGE (1988).

[9] *Id.*

[10] *Id.* The importer has two years to reclaim any duty paid on instructions, information and data content.

accepted practice in virtually every other major market in the world. Please call with any questions you may have. We thank you in advance for your kind attention to this matter. With best regards,

Sincerely,

Richard E. Neff
Legal Adviser

cc: Joseph Papovich, Deputy Ass't USTR, Intellectual Property
Robert Holleyman, President, BSA
Eric Smith, Executive Director, IIPA
Jeffrey Steinhardt, Chairman, BSA Latin America Committee
Eugenio Pallarés, Commercial Attaché, U.S. Embassy (Argentina)

RESPONSES OF ROBERT W. HOLLEYMAN II TO QUESTIONS FROM SENATOR GRASSLEY

Question 1. It is my understanding that there may be a transition period for some of the less developed and developing countries in the GATT agreement relative to intellectual property. Can you tell me what effect, if any, these transition periods will have on your individual industry . . . And which countries in particular give you the greatest concern during the transition?

Answer. BSA views the successful inclusion of the trade-related intellectual property (TRIPs) requirements in the final GATT agreement as a major victory for the software industry, and for the U.S. economy. However, BSA shares the view of our allied organizations within the International Intellectual Property Alliance (IIPA), that the existence of a four-year transition period for Less Developed Countries (LDCs) and a ten-year transition period for Least Developed Countries (LLDCs) might encourage countries (otherwise inclined to improve laws protecting intellectual property within their borders) to wait and take advantage of these transition periods. Because of the potential harm such transition periods could inflict on the software industry, BSA advocates using Special 301 and other trade programs [e.g. CBI, GSP, etc.] to accelerate the compliance of developing countries with TRIPs obligations.

BSA is particularly concerned that the Big Emerging Market (BEM) countries, if left to their own devices, will take advantage of the GATT transition periods relative to intellectual property protection. In 1993, the U.S. software industry suffered over $1.5 billion dollars in losses due to software piracy in the BEM countries. The BEM countries, as defined by Commerce Secretary Ron Brown, are: South Korea, Brazil, Mexico, Poland, Indonesia, India, Turkey, Argentina, South Africa, and the People's Republic of China.

Question 2. We have all seen countries placed on a Priority Watch List or a Watch List for its failure to enforce intellectual property rights laws and regulations. My question is how effective is naming these countries to one of these lists in having them come into compliance in your view?

Answer. Listing countries on the Priority Foreign Country, Priority Watch and Watch Lists, especially when the USTR has instituted an out-of-cycle review of that country, has been a remarkably successful means to encourage foreign governments to protect intellectual property.

Question 3. This past April USTR identified 36 trading partners that deny adequate and effective protection of intellectual property or deny fair and equitable market access to U.S. individuals that rely upon intellectual property protection. Six. countries: Japan, Korea, the European Union, Saudi Arabia, Thailand, and Turkey were either placed or retained on the "Priority Watch List" Which of these countries pose the greatest threat to your industry and why?

Answer. Of the six countries listed, Japan, Korea and Thailand pose the greatest threat to the software industry. The U.S. software industry experienced losses due to piracy of over $1.2 billion in these three countries alone. Moreover, due to weak enforcement, software piracy (of one form or another) is largely unchecked in Japan,

Korea and Thailand. In Korea, for example, government officials have been hesitant to grant ex parte searches of large institutional user believed to be using unlicensed software, similarly, in Japan, organizational end-user piracy is widespread with no clear means of addressing the problem under the Japanese legal system or expression of willingness to address the problem by the Japanese government. In Thailand retail piracy is rampant, and the Thai government has not met its commitments to strengthen enforcement against software pirates.

Question 4. I'd like to know how strong each of you feel about the need for Congress to pass a GATT agreement this year . . . Passing a budget waiver to pay for it . . . If you are a beneficiary of GATT, your willingness to shoulder a portion of the burden to pay for a portion of the $40 billion dollar cost.

Answer. The BSA strongly supports passage of the GATT this year. The TRIPs text (contained in the Uruguay Round accord) encompasses many of the provisions that the U.S. has sought over the last decade or more, including protection for software under copyright as a literary work, for a term of 50 years, coupled with enforcement obligations. These provisions will greatly enhance the U.S. software industry's ability to compete in markets worldwide. As for passing a budget waiver to pay for the implementation of the GATT, BSA has not polled its members, but does not believe that there would be any strong objection to the passage of such a waiver, if Congress determines that it is appropriate.

BSA believes that in the long-run implementation of the GATT will improve the U.S. trade balance. We expect that the U.S. software industry will flourish under the liberalized trade rules of the GATT, and will in-turn contribute more to the U.S. economy. Therefore, we do not suggest making the U.S. software industry less competitive by imposing new taxes. For obvious reasons, BSA cannot endorse the imposition of any new tax or other cost for the software industry to pay for the GATT.

○

ISBN 0-16-047078-1
90000
9 780160 470783